faster than the speed of change

faster than the speed of change

How to transform your business into a high-performance,
high-profit, high-satisfaction enterprise:
Secrets from a leading executive coach and futurist

paul lemberg

Akiba Press

Printed in the United States of America.

Published by: Akiba Press, PO Box 502612, San Diego, CA 92150-2612

Publisher's Cataloging-in-Publication
  (Provided by Quality Books, Inc.)

Lemberg, Paul
        Faster than the speed of change : how to
    transform your business into a high-performance,
    high-profit, high-satisfaction enterprise :
    secrets from leading executive coach and
    futurist / Paul Lemberg -- 1st ed.
        p. cm.
        LCCN: 00-191021
        ISBN 0-9701121-3-0

        1. Success in business. 2. Leadership.
    3. Executive ability.   I. Title

        HF5386.L46 2000   650.1
                        QBI00-548

Jacket Design by Gene Seidman
Text Design by Leslie Anne Lemberg

To my wife, Leslie,
and my many friends
who encouraged me along the way.

CONTENTS

III. FAST SPIRIT

IV. FAST TALKING

V. FAST DIRECTION

VI. FAST ACTION

ACKNOWLEDGMENTS

This book is the result of years of executive coaching and strategic consulting work with many clients. I thank them all for the opportunities to contribute to their companies, and for the things they taught me in return. In addition, I thank my wife Leslie, for her continual support and also for designing the text, Paul Myers of Talkbiz for his graceful editing of words, and Gene Seidman of Rogers/Seidman for the book's cover design. I also wish to thank Tom O'Brien and Sarah Victory for their constant encouragement.

INTRODUCTION

This is a different kind of business book.

It's a practical handbook, a detailed how-to book to help you make your business, your company, any venture at all—even your life—go faster than the speed of change.

This book is about transforming yourself and all the people within your venture into high-performance, highly focused players in an exciting and rewarding game. It is about transforming hard work into power, and transforming your visions into reality.

If you follow the steps in this book you will accomplish more, in less time, with greater profit, purpose and satisfaction.

I guarantee it.

How do you go faster than the speed of change?

With strong purpose and clear intentions. With a willingness to focus your efforts, setting everything unimportant aside. With a belief in your ability to create the future and change the world. And with the disposition to quickly admit when you've made a colossal bone-headed mistake, and turn on a dime the moment you realize it. With the courage to leap out into the unknown, and to delve into the unknowable just when you've run out of ideas.

That's how.

Sound difficult? I suppose it does when you attempt it all at once. When you try to slough off a lifetime of habits in one fell swoop—that sounds just about impossible.

It's like the old riddle:

Question: How do you get to the top of Mount Everest?
Answer: One step at a time.

When you take the steps, one by one, your Mount Everest transforms from something impossible to something you can do, just like anything else. And you make progress.

Question: How do you get to Carnegie Hall?
Answer: Practice.

This book coaches you through the practice. Take the steps one by one. Practice them, one by one, and you will create breakthroughs. Each chapter—one, two, or three pages—details a different mindset, a different way of looking at the world, a different action to take—a different way to accelerate your enterprise.

This book has a sequence, a plan, an order. It is also designed for you to pick it up at any point. Do the book in order, or do it at random. It doesn't matter at all. But do the exercises. Each piece you take action on will without a doubt—speed up your venture.

Sometimes the effect will be large, and sometimes the effect will be small. Even when the impact is only 10% more—remember that's 110% of what you have—110% times 110% times 110%—you can see how these changes—these accelerations—add up. And suddenly you are rocketing up your chosen path to the future.

Who should read this book?

If you are a corporate executive or an entrepreneur who is challenged to stay ahead of the incredible rate of change in our world (and who isn't?) this book was written explicitly for you. It provides you with a detailed operating manual for executing change in a fast-paced world.

But that begs the question: Who should read it?

Anyone.

Anyone who is intent on moving faster than the speed of change, that is. That includes corporate executives and entrepreneurs. It also includes government officials and community activists. It even includes students and homemakers, who I have had the rich experience of observing quite closely—this book can even help you make a difference.

Why read this book?

Read it because the world is moving faster and faster. And barring some cataclysmic event, it is likely to keep doing so for some time to come. Given that rate of change, your old ways of innovating and responding to innovation are no longer enough to compete and prosper. This book shows you how to transcend the pace of change and invent the future on your own terms.

This book shows you how to move faster than the speed of change.

How to use this material

There are two major reasons you might use this book.

One is that you have an ongoing business venture, and you'd simply like to speed things up and transcend the pace of change. Use the chapters in this book as a checklist. Each chapter represents an approach—a broad strategy, or maybe a self-contained tactic, which can cause a breakthrough in your business.

For instance, you may have gotten very far indeed without having a grand vision for your venture—but now that you are seeking to create breakthroughs—a vision may be just what you need. Go through the chapters, either in order or at random. You may already be implementing some of these ideas. Try the others on for size. See which fit and implement those. Skip those which are not right for you. Each strategy or tactic you don't already utilize could—all by itself—transform your business.

Think of what five or ten of these "little transformations" can do.

Then there are those of you who are starting something from scratch. Think of this as a manual—a step-by-step guide. Do as many of these chapters as you can handle. Or, take the quiz in Chapter One and use that as a road map. Read each chapter in turn, doing the exercises or actions. They will make a profound difference in the velocity and magnitude of your results.

Regardless of whether your venture is new or in full swing, do the exercises and the checklists. There is not one drop of pure theory in this book.

Simply knowing what is in here will not make you smarter. *Using* what is in here will make you much smarter and much more effective.

Remember: these tools were derived from my work with large corporations and small businesses, and apply equally to both, as well as to non-profit, government, and community projects. They apply to a small company's marketing initiative to boost sales, or to the restructuring of a global corporation. They apply to a small community project to refurbish a neighbor's house and equally well to ending world hunger. Mohandas Gandhi used these very same principals to liberate his country.

Will it work for you?

Yes. If you do the work.

If you think through the chapter, do the exercises, execute the book's prescriptions—you will produce the results you seek. This book is based on hundreds of conversations with entrepreneurs and excecutives who have repeatedly produced high levels of successes. Many of these people have been my executive coaching or consulting clients, others are simply generous souls who have been good enough to share their hard-won experience and accumulated wisdom with me.

All of this material is practical and proven. It is also workable and doable.

The Guarantee

I said earlier that I guarantee you can accelerate your results and move faster than the speed of change. I meant that.

If you do the exercises, or take the suggested actions, and for any reason find this book is not helping you or your organization go faster, please return it to me with a note, and I will refund your purchase price. (PO Box 502612, San Diego, CA 92150-2612)

Although no luck is needed to do the things suggested in these pages, I wish you Godspeed, and good luck.

Paul Lemberg

1

FAST PREPARATION

Do you still think going faster means working harder
and doing more and working harder
and doing more and...?

What if it meant something else entirely?
What if it meant having a vision of startling clarity,
maintaining a laser-like focus, and staying relentlessly on purpose?
What if it meant only doing the things which mattered to you,
and turning on a dime if your current direction isn't taking
you where you want to go?

HOW FAST DO YOU WANT TO GO?

Rank each statement 1, 2, 3 or 4 where a 1 means this statement is totally false, and a 4 means it is totally true.

The purpose of this venture is unbelievably powerful to me.

I have crystal clear objectives I intend to see accomplished.

I believe runaway success is possible and I can describe it.

Wherever things are right now, I know where to start next.

The challenge excites me.

I do what is necessary to realize to reach my purpose.

I have written specific, measurable, up-to-date objectives.

I continually take action to realize my goals and my purpose.

I am comfortable with uncertainty and ambiguity.

I spend most of my time on the most important things.

I have a definite, written action plan.

I am acting on that plan.

I track the results of my actions.

I ask people for big things.

People respond to my requests with promises and action.

I begin each day with a clear intention for that day.

I spend part of my time just thinking.

I make commitments without knowing how to fulfill them.

My business has a strategy to get through the next mission.

I know there is a chance I will fail.

I make the rules.

Quitting is not an option.

I love the game I am playing.

I can't know everything about my venture.

People around me are as inspired as I am.

If you ranked every statement "4", you would have 100 points. How did you do? What do you think it means?

You have just started this book, and already there are questions to answer and lists to make. *(You wanted fast, didn't you?)*

Right now, make a list of 10 possible short-range actions you can take immediately, which would have an important impact on your business.

1.

2.

3.

4.

5.

6.

7.

8.

9.

10.

Pick one of these actions *(for a bonus, pick two)*, write it down, and see that it is executed today.

_____

Bonus

_____

3 *DEFINING RUNAWAY SUCCESS*

To move faster than the speed of change requires a commitment to extraordinary things.

Most people, when asked for the particulars of runaway, blockbuster, or breakthrough success can't say what that means to them with enough clarity to do anything about it.

Can you?

One way to increase the pace is to consider your venture from the perspective of "runaway success," and only take actions consistent with achieving just that. Before you can do that, you have to define your terms.

Take a few moments to specify , what you would consider "runaway success" in your current venture. *(As always, there's the question of scope or context. You could say—"Well, my current venture is my life." OK—use that. If you asked me, I would suggest you narrow your scope—but it's your choice.)*

Write out your definition. You must write it out—type it— whatever. You can't simply "think" this and expect the same result. Get it out of your head and onto the page. It must reflect back to you so you can evaluate it "in the cold light of day."

Write it, in all its glory. Make sure this is a statement of "runaway success," not plain, old ordinary success.

Keep your definition in a notebook. Print it large and post it on your bulletin board. Tape it to the dashboard of your car. Slip it under your desk mat. Scatter it about your environment. Put it in your wallet where you can refer to it easily.

Then commit to making it happen.

IS IT POSSIBLE?   **4**

Is your vision of runaway success possible?

Not just for anybody—is it possible for you? Now that you have put into words the notion of runaway success—now that you know what would have you satisfied, fulfilled, inspired, and excited—do you think it is possible to achieve?

Notice—I did not ask "Do you think it is likely? Or probable?" This is not a question about the odds. Do you think it is possible —in your understanding of the world—for you or for your company?

Not "Do you know how to get it?" You may not know that now. Not "Do you have the wherewithal, or the chutzpah?" Simply—do you think, given enough time, energy, skill, knowledge and resources, you could pull it off? Is it possible for you?

This is a crucial moment in transforming your enterprise, your career, your life—your quest to move faster than the speed of change. This is the first moment of truth.

Can you make it happen?

This is a yes or no question. And the answer better be yes.

If it isn't, go back and consider some more. Without a total belief in the possibility of what you are setting out to accomplish, it isn't likely to happen. You won't go the distance. You won't do what is necessary. You won't make the sacrifices. You won't be able to inspire others or enlist their support.

You won't do the 1001 things you will be called upon to do. You might not even make it through this short, little book.

Is it possible? For you?

II

FAST THINKING

It's all about mindset.
Once you get control of that, you've got it made.

SEEING THE FUTURE   5

To manage is to lead, and to lead others requires that one enlist the emotions of others to share a vision as their own.

Henry M. Beottinger, AT&T

What is your vision of the future?

Some people think creating a vision is a complicated thing, requiring much time sequestered deep in contemplation. Others do just the opposite—they hire the job out to a consultant. Neither approach is necessary.

Having a vision is about imagining the view through the window of your future. And just as when you look out the window, you'd like the view to be warm and sunny. Inviting. Beautiful. Fulfilling.

Your well-crafted vision is all those things. It is grounded and expressed in the language of the physical world—the world of being, having and doing.

What does the future look like, what does it feel like? What is the environment? What actions are people taking? What results are being produced?

Create a complete scene, one in which you can imagine yourself. One in which other people can imagine themselves—one which inspires them. One which breathes life into your activities.

Then put it down on paper.

Create a vision statement.

The easiest way to write a vision statement is to ask questions.

**Here are twenty vision questions I ask my clients.
You can use some of these and make up your own.**

What important problems do you solve?

What unique market position do you control?

What is your geographic coverage? Are you local?
National? International? Intergalactic?

What value does your enterprise create in the world?

Is that value provided to: consumers, governments, kids, small
businesses, giant corporations, humanity?

Is your organization a corporation? A loose alliance? A strategic
partnership? A virtual company? What form is it?

Who owns the company—you? Partners? Outside investors?
The public?

How big is your organization? How many people work at/for your
company? What kind of people are they?

What role do you play daily?

How much revenue and/or profit do you generate?

What does the press say about your company?

Are you leading edge / bleeding edge / innovative or just a cash cow?

Where are your headquarters? Where are your remote offices?

What is special about working for/at your company?

How is your company growing? Sales? New product/service lines? Acquisition?

How would you describe your company culture?

What do your customers say about your company?

What is your company known for?

How do you redefine the industry you are in?

What is the future of your company?

**Important note. This is not a one-time-only process.
This can be revisited as often as necessary.**

How do you know when you need to revisit it, and create a new vision? When things start to feel routine. When the actions you are taking on a daily basis are no longer inspired, or when they begin to feel lifeless. When nothing is pulling you forward.

That's the time to invent a new vision.

6 *HAVING BIG PROBLEMS*

Small problems demand small efforts and yield small rewards. Big problems demand big efforts and yield big rewards. Have bigger problems.

Paul Lemberg

Challenging yourself—deliberately setting big (perhaps too big) problems in front of you—is a key to moving faster than change. Small challenges never lead to big successes. Challenge yourself with big problems, big issues.

The level of challenge you establish sets the level of risks you are willing to take. It sets the level of effort you are willing to put forth.

Do small problems inspire you? Of course not—they annoy you. They bog you down, and take up your time. Who would risk much for a small problem and its small reward?

Big challenges call forth the best in you. The changes you must make in rising to meet those challenges can cause an important shift in the world, and help people to be their best. There's more at stake. More to lose. More to gain.

For some people, rising to the challenge is itself a powerful reward. Rising before dawn and getting a whiff of the frosty air before a cold morning's run is by itself compensation, and makes the run that much more meaningful. The challenge adds its own joy and power to the project or program. People want to rise to the challenge—it gives them energy. It makes things more fun.

Ask yourself these questions about your business:

Is this venture a big enough challenge?
Have we bitten off more than we can chew?

If the answer is yes, that's good. If not—bite off more! What would make this a real challenge? Have we thrown down the gauntlet and dared ourselves to succeed? What would add drama? What would add scope? What would make it exciting, maybe even somewhat threatening? What would make it important?

Above all, the challenge must be important.

7

GOING NON-LINEAR

Runaway success requires that you break out of the ordinary.

Everything—and I mean everything—you are currently being and doing, the sum of all your attitudes and actions, however vigorously you pursue them, is producing results. These results follow the "normal course of events."

Research by The Conference Board suggests that for most businesses, this "normal course of events" reflects annual growth in the neighborhood of 5-10%. A straight line up and to the right, year in, year out.

On the other hand, breakthrough results are not predictable based on the way things are going. They do not occur as a matter of course. There is no logical progression from "normal" to "breakthrough."

A breakthrough occurs when, all of a sudden, your trajectory shifts dramatically. When the line of your growth is out of sync with all previous results. To create a high-speed venture, one which is growing faster than the market, changing faster than change, you must be "extra-ordinary".

By definition,

You must do something you've never done before.

Apply this picture to your business.

What would be on your curve for a "breakaway trajectory?" What kind of action and results would place you there?
What is so different, so extraordinary, that it could propel you ahead faster than change?

HOW TO MAKE BREAKTHROUGHS **8**

I would think of things I'd never thunk before...
Scarecrow, in <u>The Wizard of Oz</u>

A breakthrough occurs first in the mind.

You create breakthroughs by thinking things you haven't thought before and by doing things you haven't done before. By definition, whatever you've done up until now is factored into whatever results you've gotten. So now you're going to have to do something different.

Breakthroughs are produced by locating a space you haven't been in before, and stepping in. It could be the space of transcendental effort. It could be the space of uniquely innovative action design. Or the space of letting go—giving up control of some key process. Or the space of strategic partnerships and high-leverage relationships. Or the space of time dedicated to thinking. Or the space created by employees who have total buy-in. Or the space of powerful vision energizing all participants.

It might be anything. You don't know ahead of time. By searching the world of what you don't know and don't know that you don't know—asking the right questions and keeping your mind open to infinite possibility, you uncover the lever which lets you transform your venture into a breakthrough.

What have you "never thunk before?"

9   *THINKING FOR A CHANGE*

...And then I'd sit, and think some more.

More from the Scarecrow

How much time do you spend thinking during any given day, week or month?

I'm not thinking about the kind of thinking you do while driving in your car, commuting on the train, or while on your morning run. I'm not even thinking about the thinking you do in the shower. I'm thinking about the kind of thinking you do ensconced in your easy chair, at your desk, or in your garden. You are not reading a book or a magazine, nor watching TV, nor listening to music. You are simply thinking.

How much time do you spend doing that? Most of you will answer, none. And to that I wonder, where do your ideas come from? Moving faster than the speed of change requires great ideas, or at least a lot of good ideas.

Many people consider thinking—idle thinking at that—to be a luxury. After all, you are not really doing anything, are you? In our action-driven society we need to be doing something. Much of the time we seem to be doing two or three things. But *nothing*?

If you've never done this I urge you: THINK! You will be amazed and surprised at what can come from just thinking.

Start slowly. Set aside one hour per week for thinking. The only equipment you need is your mind and maybe a blank pad of paper and pen, or a voice recorder. Find yourself a quiet space where you can remain undisturbed. Lock your door and put a sign on it if you must. Or go to your local park and sit on a bench. Anywhere you can get away is the perfect place for thinking.

Then think. Let your mind drift, or focus on a particular problem. It's your choice. Either way, spend the entire hour thinking. Along the way, you may make notes, either written or oral. You might draw, or make mind maps. Do this for one hour a week, for one month. As you advance in this discipline—and you will like it— think for longer periods of time or set aside thinking time more often.

Here are some things to do during your thinking time.

You can consider solutions to particular problems facing your business, or consider what the problems facing your company are.

You can generate ideas.

Use the Legal Pad process. Start with a blank paper. At the top of the paper print a question about the issue under consideration.

If you are thinking about how to get new customers, ask "How can I get new customers?" Then write out AT LEAST 20 answers to the question. You have to write 20. Don't stop at 17 or 18, thinking you've done the job. And you have to write all 20 in one session.

You can use your thinking time to work on detailed strategies or plans for particular initiatives you are considering. Write outlines, position statements, visions, etc. Invent new ideas, plan your work, rehearse your speeches, review your goals.

Use your thinking time for anything you like.

You might start off by thinking about the breakthrough the Scarecrow made.

10   *DAYDREAMING*

I would while away the hours, consulting with the flowers, conferring with the rain...

The Scarecrow, yet again

For most of us, daydreaming is really out of bounds. We might believe that time set aside for focused thinking is acceptable, but idle daydreaming really goes against our type-A biases. So much so that we chastise ourselves publicly whenever we get caught—"Oh, I was just daydreaming."

Daydreaming... Hmmm. Dreamlike musings or fantasies, while awake. I must admit it doesn't sound much like work. But Einstein came up with the basis for Relativity Theory while daydreaming, and Friedrich Kekulé conceived of the carbon ring during a fanciful reverie. There are many other examples. Daydreaming has definitely proved its worth to the human race.

How does this apply to moving fast, faster than change?

Let yourself go. Give your thoughts some room to stretch out and go wild. Let your mind roam and range, inventing whatever images, sounds and feelings, stories and fanciful creations it desires. There's no pressure to come up with anything useful.

But you might.

And therein lies the opportunity. You just might come up with something far out on the curve—far ahead of whatever the market is thinking about. Something very useful—your next source of competitive advantage. You see, if your normal left brained analytical thinking hasn't given you the great idea you need, your daydreaming brain, freed from the bounds of standard reality, just might.

There is a side benefit. Daydreaming frees your mind for creative thinking later on. While you might not generate any break-through ideas during your dreaming, you may be more inventive later on. The solution to some thorny problem might pop into your mind later, because you loosened things up a bit.

Spend some quality time each week daydreaming. Give your-self an hour or so. Go to the beach, or the park, or sit in your den. Put your feet up and relax. Play some music if you like. Keep a pad or a recorder handy if you want to make some notes.

Let your mind wander. Who knows what it'll come up with?

11   *BEING WRONG*

What if you're wrong?

What if that brilliant idea you've just hatched is totally hare-brained and never going to work?

Many of us assume we are right, and that our thoughts are spot-on. We get defensive when others suggest we might be off base.

If you're going to move fast, you're going to have to take some risks in your thinking. Be willing to criticize your own ideas. Be open to finding fault with all your wonderful brainstorms. Look for the loopholes. Look for the mistakes. You might even invite those around you to take pot shots at your ideas.

Some ways to criticize your own ideas:

Imagine you are wrong. (Horrors!) What then? What would being wrong cause to happen, and what are some ways around these problems?

Sidestep. What else is like what you are doing? If this part of your venture is flawed, where else has similar logic caused you to go astray, with problems lying undiscovered? How will you deal with those issues when they surface?

What have you forgotten? What have you left out?

What if it's just too big and you made it smaller? Or larger? What if it needs to be slower, or faster? A bit sooner, or perhaps later? What if you made the whole thing flashier, pumped up the volume, and turned up the heat? What if you made it more subtle, quieter?

All of these questions flow from being willing to be wrong. All of these questions can have the effect of making you more flexible in your thinking—the key to having an organization not only responsive to change—but one which anticipates change.

So, what if you're wrong?

BELIEVE IT OR NOT! **12**

Do you believe you can get out in front of a changing market, and stay there? Or do you believe the rate of change will ultimately render your company uncompetitive? It's your choice, take your pick.

I know this is a bold statement—but the first constraint on your ability to perform is the belief you hold about your ability to perform. If you don't believe something is possible, will you try? If you believe you can be so intuitive and flexible that you can achieve that Holy Grail—*sustainable competitive advantage*—at least you have a chance.

You will only go as far as you believe you can. And not one inch further. Your beliefs have absolute power over your actions.

Think about it for a moment. The things you hold to be true or false govern the type of actions you take. If you think something is a foregone conclusion, you are not going to waste effort to prevent it, or expend effort to make it happen. Why would you, it's going to happen anyway, despite your efforts pro or con.

If you think you are doomed to failure, how will that affect the energy you put into your business?

If you believe you will surely succeed, might that cause you to go into overdrive?

You can use your beliefs to take control of change in your industry. The first step is to gain clarity about what you believe, instead of having your personal truths operating hidden in the background.

What are your beliefs about your current venture? Ask yourself, what do I believe about _____? *(You may specifically question your beliefs about your ability to cope with change.)*

Write each belief below, or on a separate sheet of paper.

I believe:

I believe:

I believe:

I believe:

I believe:

I believe:

I believe:

I believe:

I believe:

I believe:

Examine these beliefs you have just written. Think about what they imply.

What kind of choices will having these beliefs cause you to make? What kind of actions will they prevent? Some beliefs strengthen your venture, increasing the likelihood of high-speed success. Some beliefs weaken it, sucking power from your efforts, holding you back from purposeful action.

This is a critical juncture for your enterprise. You've got to stack the deck in your favor if you want your company to be on the move. Beliefs are not carved in stone. You are not stuck with "bad" beliefs. You can modify them just as you can modify your value system.

Carefully consider each belief, and label each one with a "+" or a "-". You are going to do a little head work.

You are going to alter your beliefs about yourself and your business.

First, declare the possibility of altering your beliefs. You must truly believe that you can change your limiting ideas, replace them with more powerful and enabling belief systems.

Next, strengthen your positive beliefs.

For each one, visualize that belief. Form a picture of the consequences of this belief. What does this belief portend for the future of your operation? Create a bright, colorful, image of that. Hold onto that image, gaze at it. Picture yourself as part of it, up close and personal. Make your whole body resonate with this belief.

Got it? OK, on to the next belief. Keep this up until you have created a strong sensation for each of your positive beliefs.

Now, one by one, for each negative belief, decide what positive belief would be useful to substitute. Write that new, positive belief next to the old, negative belief.

Consider the negative belief. Picture it in your mind as you did before. Only this time you are going to detach yourself from it. Picture it from a distance, outside looking in, in muddy, dim colors or black and white. Make any sounds you hear faint and unclear. Shake off any feelings these beliefs give you, as if they are simply unreal.

Picture the new, positive belief you are replacing it with. Hold this new belief in your mind's eye and strengthen the experience of the new belief, just as you did above with your original positive beliefs.

Do this for each of your beliefs, one at a time. You may have to repeat the exercise several times before the new beliefs totally take hold.

Your new beliefs unlock the gate to the kind of massive action your business requires to move faster than the speed of change.

Don't neglect this. The moment you realize that you truly are in control of your beliefs is an incredible breakthrough itself.

13   *FAITH*

Ya gotta have faith.   George Michaels

Faith is absolutely essential to creating a breakthrough for your enterprise. Specifically, faith that your venture and its vision will be realized. Faith means unshakable confidence, total trusting acceptance.

Faith puts you beyond doubt, in the realm of complete certainty. Once in that realm you are willing to try anything, do anything necessary to realize your vision. To have your dreams come true.

At the margins, there are many actions you are unlikely to take if you weigh the likelihood of success and failure. On the other hand, if you know, absolutely know, things will work out—those marginal actions don't seem marginal anymore. They simply make sense. Breakthroughs are often the result of action at the margin of reasonableness. So faith has a way of keeping us in action, keeping us ahead of the change curve.

How do you develop faith? This is tough to swallow, but you just have to "have" it. Faith is a declaration you make to yourself. You simply say, "I have total faith in this and such." And then you have it. You say "I have faith" and then you take action based upon your faith. When the voice in your head raises doubts about your outcome, you counter with your faith in the outcome. Over and over again if necessary.

You keep keeping the faith.

Take in a deep breath, and let it out slowly and say "I declare that I have absolute, total, unshakable faith in

_____."

Doesn't that feel good?

What if it doesn't work?

Who hasn't had such thoughts? "It won't work. It isn't right. They won't like it. It will fail." And in more insidious, more personal forms: "I'm not good enough. I will fail."

Who hasn't thought such thoughts when you are smack dab in the middle of the most important thing you've ever done?

Doubt is part of the human condition. If you are functioning on a high level, working far outside your comfort zone, doubt is inevitable. After all—you are working in realms with which you are unfamiliar. Perhaps you really don't know what you're doing.

Uncertainty that you will reach your destination is logical when sailing uncharted waters. But if you were familiar with the terrain and had all the knowledge necessary, you wouldn't be on the verge of a breakthrough. You certainly wouldn't be outrunning change.

Doubt can stop you dead in your tracks; cause you to seize up and cease action. "Oh my God, I can't go on. I'm all wrong. I'm bound to fail."

What if you could have thoughts like these and keep going? Can you have doubt—grave doubt—and still do what you have to?

Of course you can! The problem is that most people think their doubts must be paid attention to, that they reflect reality.

They don't.

There are two types of doubt. The first is what I'll call "technological doubt"—doubt about your approach and your methods. This kind of doubt can serve a positive purpose, causing you to double-check, to think through your plans and make sure you are taking your best shot.

The other is "fearful doubt"—the automatic human response to anything that places you out on a limb. Ignore this doubt. Trust your gut to tell you the difference.

Acknowledge that you have doubts, embrace them as part of your humanity—then suck it up and keep going. Even though these doubts may make your stomach hurt—keep doing whatever it is you said you had to do next.

Like many things, you don't have to like doubt, it doesn't have to feel good, and it doesn't have to get in your way.

Doubt is very effective at keeping you behind the curve. Let others be out on the bleeding edge. Let others take the arrows. Things are changing so fast, let's wait and see. Right?

It's a fact—if you are going to run your business as an innovator—you're going to have to face doubt, and lots of it. You may not have it personally—but your people or your partners will. The only question is, how are you going to deal with it?

Make another list. This time, make a list of your doubts. Don't be shy. Write them out on paper, one after the next, for all your consciousness to see. Exhaust the list. Acknowledge you have such doubts, that they are part of your human heritage.

Throw the list away.

Now, get back to doing whatever it was you were doing.

REFLECTION 15

Take time out for reflection. Examine your experiences and learn what there is to learn.

The very act carries with it the notion of slowing things down, as if you had all the time in the world. Mostly we are so busy pushing things forward we don't take stock of where we are. We don't take time to reckon our location, or to acknowledge our progress. Reflection is a way to counterbalance the accelerated pace of change. Reflection grounds you in the certainty of the moment.

Take a deep breath. Stop time for a moment.

Reflect on the business you're creating and the life you're living. What have you accomplished? View this with your inner eye.

What have you learned? Whom have you met? What have you seen? How has it changed you? Who are you being as you expand your venture's horizons?

Who are you—right now?

Make time on a regular basis for reflection. Set aside an hour or two a week for the purpose of reflecting. You might later expand to 1/2 hour a day. Just think things through.

Or start a journal and make notes about what has happened—not as a work of literature, but as a simple record. A way to mark the path you are on and detail some of the sights.

Another approach is to spend some time each evening just remembering what has transpired. Begin at the end, right where you are, and work your way backward to when your day started.

Choose an approach that gives you the greatest insight, then use it.

See yourself in your reflection.

16   *AN INTERIM SELF-ASSESSMENT*

Take this test to find out if you are ready to pilot your business at the speed of change. Or faster.

Can you live with uncertainty?

Do you enjoy taking risks?

Are you self-confident?

Are you persistent?

Do you set goals and follow through to achieve them?

Can you turn on a dime?

Do you learn from your failures and mistakes?

Can you make important decisions quickly?

Can you say you were wrong and change your mind, quickly?

Do you keep your word with respect to your commitments?

Can you take charge, and take the heat?

Do you enjoy the challenge?

Do you require security and stability?

Can you imagine that you see the future?

For each "yes", give yourself 10 points. For each no, you had better figure out how to turn it into a yes if you want your business to be a runaway success.

When you have 120 points, go for it.

NO-PROBLEM ZONE **17**

Reduce the friction and drag that problems cause. Establish your venture as a no-problem zone.

That doesn't mean things never go wrong for you. It means that you don't hang on to the wrongness; you don't worry about whether things should be the way they are; and you don't wallow in the problem state.

You discover you have a problem, and set about making the things which are wrong right again.

Here is a little drill which will aid you in turning your venture into a no-problem zone. This is best done out loud with someone else—maybe one of your co-adventurers, or an advisor. If you do this yourself, write out your responses for some objectivity.

What is the "problem"?

Who is this a problem for?

What about what happened makes this seem like a problem for *you?*

Restate the problem, and also restate the commitment behind this problem.

Declare that there is no problem.

State the "problem" as a new commitment.

Is that commitment consistent with your overall vision and objectives?

Invent three new actions to bring that commitment to reality.

Take action.

See? No problem.

18

INFORMATION

We live in an information age, yet most of us try to limit our exposure to new information to our specialized areas of interest.

One way to accelerate beyond change is to 1] uncover knowledge you didn't know you didn't have, and 2] act on that new knowledge.

Knowledge is information plus insight—so the raw fuel for outrunning change is information. Breakthroughs thrive on fresh information. To stay out ahead of the curve, you need a steady flow of it.

Read regularly. The obvious things to read are trade publications, newsletters, and digests, along with books about your field. Then there are books outside your field, which may be more important in terms of fostering insight and mental leaps. Haphazardly surfing the Internet is a terrific way of stumbling across information you didn't know you were looking for.

Attend conferences, both the regional and national events, as well as local breakfast and after-hours events. Go both for the speakers and the networking chit-chat.

Read national newspapers, but don't worry about the news. Look at the small filler articles. That's were the best stuff is. The same is true for the general business publications. You may not care about the big cover stories, but the inside articles are often gems.

Another great source of industry information is prospective employees. Interviews yield all sorts of scuttlebutt, and while this is mostly rumor, even good rumors may be useful to you.

Keep up the flow. If you don't read now, start. If you read magazines but have no time for books, make some.

Get as much information as you can.

KNOWLEDGE **19**

So now you have a steady flow of information. But information isn't enough.

New knowledge is what you need to stay ahead of the curve. How do you turn the information into knowledge?

By asking questions to gain insight.

When I was about seven or eight years old, my father would tell me to look words up in the dictionary. The problem was I was such a bad speller I didn't know where to look. Very frustrating indeed.

This knowledge process is a bit like that. If you don't know what you don't know, how are you going to ask a question about it? What information are you going to access?

It's not as tough as it seems.

When most people read, or listen to a speaker at a conference, they're gathering information. Recording facts, figures, war stories, that sort of thing. They typically lack focus; they don't have a goal for the reading or the listening.

To create new knowledge you have to do something else—you have to deliberately identify the areas you are interested in—your areas of concern.

Use your concern as a way to focus. Express the concern to yourself and it becomes a lightning rod for insight and knowledge. As you read or listen, watch TV or surf the web, or have conversations, the concern operates in the background—searching and sifting— making relevant connections, new distinctions, and finally insight.

If you define your outcome in concrete terms, your mind will give you the solution.

More "How to know what you don't know"

Another way to get an idea of what you don't know that you don't know is to answer the following short list of questions. Don't limit yourself to situations in your own field. Often the best solutions are those that others in your field don't know about.

First, choose a situation and ask yourself

"What results do others get that I don't, but should?"

For each outcome, answer the following:

What do they need to know to get those results?
What do they need to do to get those results?
What resources, systems and contacts are needed to get those results?
What do I need to do to find out?

And then the most important question...

How can I apply this directly to my own situation?

You know that moment when a flash of brilliance bursts into your awareness. It's incredible!

But you can't depend on flashes. Although they happen, you might end up waiting a long time.

Another way to find these revolutionary ideas is to look at the world as it is, and deliberately invent a new way for it to be.

Now you have a new idea. But you will want to validate it. Is this a good idea? Can you build a business on this idea?

Research lets you answer these and other questions.

The thought of research scares people. It conjures images of expensive marketing consultants going door to door, or a bank of telemarketers calling people at dinner time.

Well, the scale may be different, but the concept *is* the same. Much of market research is talking to people. Call people you know, ask them whether your idea would be of any use to them. If you don't know any one who would use your product or service, ask people who they know.

Network. Talk to individuals representing at least ten organizations. That's a minimum but not totally reliable. Thirty organizations will give you a strong foundation. Ask those people if they'd buy your "thing," and at what price they'd buy it. Ask them what features it should have other than the ones you've already mentioned.

Next you have to determine how many potential customers exist for your product. Describe the type of person or organization who would consume your product.

Can you describe them demographically? By age, sex, job description, geography, income bracket, industry type, etc.? If not, who are they most similar to? What similar thing do they already buy which is measured? What publications do they all read? You have to find *something* you can count.

Now you know the size of your potential market.

After you count them, you need to make another guess: what percentage will buy. That is the potential for your product.

If you want to go the next step, make a test offer. Write a letter—create a promotion and test mail it to a segment of the population you've identified. Or call them on the phone, if the number is small enough. Invite them to use your product.

Keep refining the details of your offer until a large enough number say yes.

Congratulations. You've just done market research, the fast way. Now you can rush full speed ahead into product development knowing there is a market for your ideas.

And the only consultants you needed were your customers.

I had six honest serving men, they taught me all I know, their names were who, and what, and when, and where, and why, and how.

Rudyard Kipling

Kipling's ditty is also known as the Journalist's Credo. The lead paragraph of just about any newspaper story answers each of these six questions. So should the plan for any initiative or venture—large or small.

These six questions can teach you a lot as well. Once past the germ of an idea, but certainly before execution, you must answer each one of these six simple questions. Some of these questions have to be answered several times.

Who—will do the work, will benefit from the work, will pay for the work?

When—will it begin, and/or, when will it finish?

What—exactly is being planned? What will be the outcome?

Where—is it being done? Where will it be sold?

Why—is this being done? Why will someone buy it?

How—will it be done?

No matter what the project, each of Kipling's serving men must be addressed. Take each one in turn and ask as many questions as possible using each one.

Who

What

Where

Why

How

When

Another way for these six to serve you is to apply them to any situation where you seem stuck. Just start asking the questions. Who? What? Et cetera.

You'll be surprised what they can teach you.

Have you ever had an un-meeting of the minds?

When was the last time you and your team spent time just thinking—together? When did you get out of the office and sit around for a day, or even two, mulling things over?

I don't mean playing golf or climbing a ropes course. Just hanging out—in a hotel or someone's backyard. Examining where you've been and where you'd like to go. And maybe how you might get there.

Take a day every three months. Or 2 days twice a year. Spend enough time to really get into it. What is your vision? Is it still valid? What strategy have you been pursuing? Is it paying off? Should you revamp the whole thing?

Ask yourselves some of the following questions. Make sure you get good answers. Encourage everyone's participation. Don't let people hide out.

What have you been trying to accomplish?

What have you been doing that works?

What have you been doing that doesn't work?

What is missing from what you are doing?

What do you want to do next?

What will it take that you don't already have?

What is the plan for getting to the next stage?

Who is going to do what?

Who will be responsible for what?

Meetings are set to achieve pre-defined goals. Un-meetings are set to decide what the goals should be. Meetings are tolerated. Un-meetings are celebrated.

Take a leap forward. Have an un-meeting.

SHARING YOUR VISION **23**

The task of the leader is to get his people from where they are to where they have not been…Leaders must invoke the alchemy of great vision.
Henry Kissinger

Why shared vision?

Isn't the founder's or chief executive's or your vision good enough? Well yes, but when your people "share" the vision, it becomes theirs. If they own it, they'll care for it, work for it, and live for it, just as though it were theirs alone.

Here is a process for creating a shared vision.

1. Have each team member articulate his or her vision. You can write them out ahead of time, or do it on the spot. Either way, have them all written out and visible.

2. Spend time talking about where you want to go as a team. Let people speak their piece, and include their personal future as well as the company future. Have people say how the two are intertwined.

3. Next, create a list of key words or phrases that express your individual and collective visions. Write them on a board or flipchart—as many as it takes to capture what everyone has to say. Don't worry about repetition, or even contradiction.

4. If you are more than eight people, break into groups of four to six. Each group weaves the key words and phrases into one or two paragraphs which express the group's vision. You need not use every word, just the expressive ones. Each member of the group has to agree and be complete with the final statement.

5. If you have broken into groups, each group displays their "vision" and reads it aloud. All present vote on which statement expresses the vision in the most empowering and accurate way. If there is a tie (or near tie) find a way to merge the competing visions. Look for creative and inspired compromise.

If individuals need particular additions or deletions to make the final choice work—do those in a way which satisfies the entire group.

You are done when your entire team—this can be two people or two hundred—embrace your shared vision, and sees it as their own.

That's a powerful place to be.

III

FAST SPIRIT

Your purpose and your values.

What you commit to, and what you are responsible for.

These things form the core of your existence.

They shape who you are, they define what you are capable of.

They are the spirit of your enterprise, providing vitality and vigor.

ALL THINGS FLOW FROM THE SOURCE **24**

Face it. You are the source of your project, your venture, your enterprise. Whatever it is, it comes from you. That's the nature of leadership.

This is true whether or not you conceived the idea. It is true whether or not someone higher up the chain asked you *(or ordered you)* to do it. It is true whether or not you wanted to be the leader.

Once you've assumed the mantle of leadership, you are the source.

How do you "be" the source?

By saying it. "I am the source." By thinking it. By *standing* as the source—which means looking at things from that perspective. How would your business look to you, what would you see, think, feel—and do—if you were standing at the source of things.

Make that perspective your perspective.

OK—take that on. Stand there, at the head of your venture, just like standing at the head of a river. Stand at the source and "be" the source. Have the whole thing flow from you. Whatever happens along the way, it will, at a very fundamental level, come from you.

Can you do that?

This is not about your ego. This is not "Look at me, I'm the source. This thing comes from me." This is a commitment thing. Willingness to be the source is the nature of responsibility. You are the source and cause of whatever actions are being taken and whatever results are being produced.

As a leader, you are responsible. You are the source.

25 *THE FAMILY JEWELS*

There is a lot of talk in our society about values.

Family values, personal values, corporate values. What are values and why are they important to creating breakthroughs?

Values are things we strive to gain or keep. They are the expression of what is important to us. Values can be concrete things like money, gourmet food, and fast motorcycles, or they can be abstract things like contribution, challenge, or adventure. Your values are truly "the family jewels".

Values, along with our beliefs about what will satisfy our values, have a decisive impact on the choices we make. We make decisions based on our values. By definition, we evaluate.

If we believe a proposed action will give us more of what we value, we are likely to take that action. And the degree to which we are likely to take that action is proportional to the strength of our beliefs and how much we think the value will increase.

We are constantly evaluating whether something is good for us or bad for us—in fact, we can't help it. It's part of our design as human beings.

A hidden value system will cause you to make choices that are inexplicable—you will choose Option A over Option B even though A seems logical. Why? Because B violates your unconscious value system.

You can use a consciously constructed values system to help turn your venture into a high performance machine. A lucid value system, out in the open—and arranged hierarchically—this is more important than that, and so on—turned into a values statement—serves as a guide in evaluating your options, and inventing new ones.

In other words, if you understand the values that motivate you, you can deliberately choose actions which will satisfy those values. Which make you feel good, and keep you conflict-free, and internally consistent. You reduce or eliminate your personal friction, allowing you to easily take massive action towards your objectives.

Your values statement also helps you align your various stakeholders, and have them act in that same consistent way.

Your values system also keeps you from making poor choices, which would throw you into personal conflict. Choices which make you unhappy and gum up the works.

(This section on values is the longest section in this book. It is valuable and worth working your way through. Well-understood and clearly expressed values can propel you through the most difficult change periods, and keep you far ahead of the wandering herd.)

Here is a list of common (and uncommon) values. This list is neither complete nor definitive. It is a guide. Please add your own.

Acceptance
Achievement
Adventure
Affection
Art
Beauty
Being Different
Challenge
Change
Commitment

Compassion
Competition
Confrontation
Contribution
Courage
Creativity
Detachment
Ecstasy
Efficiency
Ethics

Excellence

Excitement

Fame

Free Time

Freedom

God

Growth

Happiness

Hard Work

Harmony

Health

Honesty

Integrity

Knowledge

Leadership

Learning

Love

Loyalty

Making a difference

Merit

Nature

Partnership

Passion

Peace

Play

Power

Prosperity

Resilience

Security

Self-awareness

Self-expression

Self-respect

Serenity

Service

Sharing

Sophistication

Stability

Success

Support

Teamwork

Trust

Truth

Wealth

Winning

Wisdom

UNDERSTANDING YOUR VALUES **26**

Define your values.

Pick an area you are working on. This could be your venture, your relationship, your profession, your LIFE.

▣ Ask "what is important to you about _____?" List all the things that come to mind.

▣ Keep asking the question—"and what else is important..?" until you believe you have exhausted the possibilities.

▣ Refer to the values list above if you get stuck. It will stimulate your thinking—have you left anything out?

▣ For each of the values on your list, ask what is important about that, and what would having more of that give me (us.)

▣ Check to see if these are things you really care about or if you just think you should care about them.

1.	11.
2.	12.
3.	13.
4.	14.
5.	15.
6.	16.
7.	17.
8.	18.
9.	19.
10.	20.

STEP 2

Now you're going to prioritize them.

◉ Start with value #1 and compare it to #2. Ask "Is this value more important than that?" and so on. How do you decide? You "look inside" and feel them. Which one matters more? This may sound strange at first, but you'll be able to tell.

◉ If #1 is more important than #2, compare it to #3. If #3 is more important, compare it to #4, #5, etc., until you reach the end of your list. The value which "wins" the final comparison goes at the top of your prioritized values list.

◉ Keep repeating this process, starting at the top of the original list, skipping the values you've already moved to the new list any previous times through. Do it until all values from the first list have a place on the second.

Prioritized Values List

1.	11.
2.	12.
3.	13.
4.	14.
5.	15.
6.	16.
7.	17.
8.	18.
9.	19.
10.	20.

Got them all in order? Good.

Now that you have been working with these and thinking about them—how do you feel about them? Does this list feel right? Do these values make you "stir" inside when you read them?

If so, you've done a good job. If not, go back and make adjustments —additions, deletions. Move things around until your list feels right.

You may have to make several passes at this. Don't quit. Keep it up until the list sings to you.

STEP 3

Write each value, followed by the "rules" for that value.

What things tell you if the value is being satisfied? For example: You have a value called Teamwork. Your rule for teamwork might be: "Teamwork is when everyone is pulling towards a common cause, without fighting."

Once you have written a rule, make sure the value is attainable. Could it be that you've created a value, and a rule for its attainment, which means you can never have that value in your life?

If your rule for teamwork is "There is no self-interest, and there are never any arguments," you will probably never have the feeling of teamwork to inspire you.

Do this for the top 8 values on your list.

Value Rules—how you know when that value is satisfied.

Value	Rule
1.	
2.	
3.	
4.	
5.	
6.	
7.	
8.	

Optional step for groups:

Once steps 1-3 are complete, get the group together.

In turn, one value at a time, each member acts out his values, using any methods at his disposal. His goal is to bring the value into existence for the rest of the group. The rest of the group can provide feedback and coaching.

STEP 4

For each value, develop a set of practices or disciplines which cement this value in place, and provide satisfaction and fulfillment regularly. For instance, to deepen your "creativity" value, you might begin a practice of drawing for two hours a week, or writing daily in a journal. Perhaps "clarity" is a value you'd like to focus on, you might meditate daily for fifteen minutes.

Value	Practices
1.	
2.	
3.	
4.	
5.	
6.	
7.	
8.	

A clearly defined set of values is essential for maintaining integrity.

Integrity, and the consistency that goes with it, are key ingredients in success of any kind. They let people know where they stand, and prevent the worst kinds of speed bumps.

They're absolutely essential for moving *"faster than change."*

Reach beyond your grasp. Your goals should be grand enough to get the best of you.

Teilhard de Chardin

Why?

Why are you doing what you're doing? Why are you pursuing this venture? Why are you even reading this book?

Why are you living your life?

The answer to these questions is your purpose. The fundamental reason for your activities.

Every truly powerful venture has a clear and motivating purpose. Why?

Why should we care about why?

Why, indeed? A powerful purpose will keep you going on days when the weather is lousy and your children kept you up all night and the dog was barking and there's no cream for the coffee and the car has a flat tire and your key person called in sick and your best customer just cancelled and the toilets are backed up....

A powerful purpose enables you to keep going and cause more breakthroughs. Without a powerful purpose you might as well go home and pull the covers over your head.

A powerful purpose provides the fuel to do whatever it takes— no matter what. It's better than strong coffee for working long hours and weekends.

A powerful purpose makes it a no-brainer to make big commitments and outsized requests, to take risky actions and put yourself on the line. Plus, your associates and employees—all the other stakeholders in your venture—need your powerful purpose as well.

Your shared purpose keeps them in the game right along with you. Purpose, along with shared vision, is the foundation of ownership—if people have a sense of purpose they will take responsibility well beyond their accountability.

How do you get a big purpose? For some people, it's just there. Like Don Quixote, you may be on a quest. Perhaps you are born with it, or it comes to you in a dream, or while you are stuck in traffic.

Sometimes you have to work to define it.

What is your purpose?

Purpose

Write down why you do what you do.

Then ask why is that important, and why do you do that. Then ask why that is important. And so on. Don't stop with the first level of reasons. It is usually necessary to keep going for a while.

When you reach bedrock "purpose" and you resonate with it— that's the one. Work on the words for a while until it really sings for you.

What I do:

Why that is important :

And why that is important :

And why that is important :

And why that is important :

And why that is important :

And why that is important :

And why that is important :

And why that is important :

State your purpose. *Out loud.* Right now. Don't be embarrassed or feel funny if you are alone. Just try it out. How does it sound? If someone else is nearby, try it out on them. Say, "I've been thinking about my purpose. Here it is," or something like that.

Many people turn their purposes into purpose statements which are short and easy to say, and inspire themselves and their stakeholders.

Here are a few famous ones:

To strengthen the social fabric by continually democratizing home ownership.	**Fannie Mae**
To give unlimited opportunity to women.	**Mary Kay**
To experience the emotion of competition, winning and crushing competitors.	**Nike**
To experience the joy of advancing and applying technology for the benefit of the public.	**Sony**
To give ordinary folks the chance to buy the same things as rich people.	**Wal-Mart**
To preserve and improve human life.	**Merck**

Can you state your purpose?

Your purpose defines your intentions, which decide your actions.

In exploring the heart of runaway success, the following questions arise: What do you intend to cause in the world? What have you decided to be responsible for?

Your intentions are the design—the planned realization of your purpose.

Complete the following sentences:

My purpose is:

I am really going to:

I am fully responsible for:

I intend to cause:

Stay on this page until you are able to finish these lines.

Out of your intentions flow your objectives, your measures, your goals and your actions—your whole game plan flows from your intentions.

If you're focused, and keep to your direction, you'll move faster than the speed of change.

CHOOSE YOUR POISON **30**

Are you in it for the short term, or the long haul?

I'm going to go a little bit out on a limb here. I'm going to suggest that very little which is worth leading a group to accomplish is going to be accomplished without discipline.

Not in the trivial things. I'm talking about the things that matter. The things that take the concerted effort of a team working together.

What kind of discipline? How about a working definition:

Doing what you know you need to do, for as long as you need to do it.

The kind of discipline which lets people hone their skills and become proficient at their jobs. The kind of discipline which enables us to adhere to standards even when it might be uncomfortable.

The kind of discipline which enables us as leaders to hold our people to account. No matter what.

There's an alternative to discipline, and it's not pretty.

It's called regret.

Regret is what you get when you knew what needed to be done and you didn't do it. Regret is what's left when you look back on your unfulfilled intentions and know you just didn't have the nerve or the commitment to bring them to life.

So there's a choice. You can have the pain of discipline—because discipline isn't easy (that's why it's called discipline) and sometimes it hurts. Or you can have the pain of regret, which never hurts in the present, but sure will feel terrible later.

And you have it for the rest of your life.

31 *BREAKTHROUGH SATISFACTION*

There is a trick to gaining terrific satisfaction in your business and your life. William Shakespeare summed it up nicely:

This above all: to thine own self be true.

First, figure out who you are in the world, and be that person, really, really, well. Master being that person.

Determine the key distinctions of being you. Then make your business an extension of yourself—have it realize your purpose, your vision, your values, and your standards at their highest level.

When your venture is an integral expression of your core being, you are joyously compelled to do everything necessary to bring it to fruition.

Can you think of a better guarantee of success?

If who you currently are isn't satisfying to you, a business fulfilling that you won't be either. And while it is still possible for it to be a financial success, it is likely not to be any fun, and not something you will want to do for very long.

If that is the case, your next step is to choose who you do want to be.

Do a gap analysis—list the important differences between how you manifest yourself in the world now, and how you want to manifest.

Develop "creative tension" between these two states, map a path from one to the next, and take concentrated action to bring that new person into existence. Master being that person, and make your operation an extension of that person.

The personal route to meaningful success is to and through your highest expression...

Be the very best of who you are going to be in the world.

IV

FAST TALKING

In the beginning there was the word.
And by the power of the word, the world was created.

COMMITMENT 32

The best bit of writing I've read on the subject of commitment comes in the following passage from a little-known book called <u>The Scottish Himalayan Expedition</u>, by W.H. Murray.

"Until one is committed, there is hesitancy, the chance to draw back, always ineffectiveness. Concerning all acts of initiative there is one elementary truth, the ignorance of which kills countless ideas and splendid plans: that the moment one definitely commits oneself then Providence moves too.

All sorts of things occur to help one that would otherwise never have occurred. A whole stream of events issues from the decision, raising in one's favor all manner of incidents and meetings and material assistance which no man would have believed would have come his way.

I have learned a deep respect for one of Goethe's couplets:

Whatever you can do, or dream you can, begin it.
Boldness has genius, power and magic in it!"

33 *DECLARING BREAKTHROUGHS*

You ought to be committed.

A key part of generating breakthrough results is simply saying you are going to generate breakthrough results. In fact, declaring an intention to have a breakthrough can precipitate taking actions that carry you past your previous limitations.

But you have to do it out loud.

There's no use telling yourself quietly that you are going to do something bold. (Isn't that a curious picture?) You have to go public. You have to declare it.

You have to commit yourself.

So, regardless of the nature of the breakthrough—general or specific—you have to declare, out loud, in a very committed and public way—your plans, your intention to have a breakthrough.

Why? Because just as W.H. Murray says about commitment, your public declaration energizes the people around you, and mobilizes forces in your favor. People become inspired and activated by the idea of doing something unprecedented and distinguished.

This extra bit of "juice" can, all by itself, push things right over the edge. Your declaration causes a shift in the world—a new possibility is created and resources and things are mobilized which simply did not seem available before.

What do you want to cause a breakthrough in?

Now say: "I intend to cause a breakthrough in

_____."

Say it like you mean it.

Fear is the mind killer.   Frank Herbert, Dune

The only fear that matters is your fear of failure.

All other fears are ultimately revealed as variants of this one. Fear of failure is the number one killer of rapid growth. Sometimes, any growth at all.

If you are afraid your venture is going to fail, you will hesitate to risk all that must be risked for its success. At some point you weigh the rewards and the costs—the rewards seem too distant and the costs too great. So you stop.

The antidote is fearlessness.

Not being afraid... A tall order and very difficult to manage, since fear is such a basic part of the human condition. How can you manage fearlessness?

You need to know, with certainty, your venture may fail. Irrespective of your faith and your beliefs about success—your venture may fail. Most certainly, it will not turn out the way you planned. Most certainly, it will not turn out the way you think it should.

Yet, because it is so important to you, because its impact is so fraught with possibility, you are willing to risk everything, do everything there is to do to make it happen anyway.

If you can master this paradox, knowing you will fail and going forward anyway—you have transformed your fear of failure into certainty about failure, and you don't give a damn.

When you know you might fail, and you courageously, faithfully go forth, that is being fearless.

Say the following:

I know this venture may fail. No matter who I am, what I risk and what I do, this venture may fail.

Knowing what you now know, are you willing to continue? Are you willing to "do whatever it takes" to realize your vision?

If so, my friend, you have become fearless.

TALK, TALK, TALK **35**

Talk is cheap. (You've heard that, haven't you?)

Yes, talk is cheap. At least most of our talk is. Cheap and meaningless. Filled with opinions, judgments, gossip, whining, and complaining.

Spend some time characterizing what is coming out of your mouth. How much of it falls into the categories listed above?

There's another kind of talk that's not cheap. It's a special way of talking designed to produce results. It consists of requests, promises, declarations and straight reporting. Cheap talk produces nothing but more cheap talk. Opinions beget more opinions. Gossip begets more gossip.

Not-cheap talk—Action Talk—is a powerful form of expression with the ability to make something happen.

Action talk contains the following elements:

Requests—asking for something specific.

Promises—a commitment to do something specific, in a certain way, by a certain time.

Declaration—a formal statement announcing the possibility of something, the existence of something, or your intention to do something.

Reports—just the facts; without opinions, assessments, judgements, or evaluations.

Be aware of the kinds of language that come out of people's mouths. You'll notice right away that the effective people you know tend to make more promises and requests, and keep their "cheap talk" to a minimum.

When they are expressing opinions or judgments they label them so.

Do this:

For the next seven days, be mindful of what kind of speaking comes out of your mouth. See if you can keep all your communication to Action Talk.

If there is something your enterprise needs, *ask for it*. If someone asks you for something, and it works for you, *promise*. If you need to communicate the facts, report them. If you want to inspire people and create a new possibility, *declare it*.

If you catch yourself opining, judging, gossiping, or any of the kinds other cheap talking—just stop. Say, "You know, that's not really what I wanted to say... ."

Talk action, and watch how much faster things happen.

BE UNREASONABLE **36**

The reasonable man adapts himself to the world; the unreasonable one persists in trying to adapt the world to himself. Therefore, all progress depends on the unreasonable man.

George Bernard Shaw—<u>Maxims for Revolutionists</u>

Nothing much happens until you make a request and ask someone to do something. But what really makes things go are requests that are "unreasonable."

What is an unreasonable request? Asking people to do things you have no right to expect from them. Asking for things you expect people to say no to. But asking anyway.

The trick is to expect them to say yes, and not worry about whether they do or they don't.

Create a game in your enterprise. The game is for everyone to continually be unreasonable in what you ask of each other, and in what you ask all your outside stakeholders. Do you think that could rocket your project or your business forward? Of course it would.

If making requests is not a normal activity for most people in businesses, unreasonable requests are doubly abnormal. We don't want to risk rejection, so we ask for small things, easy things, wimpy things, and make it easy for people to say yes.

This is a good strategy if you are no-o-phobic, but it limits your results.

The action in your business is moved forward in direct proportion to the size of your requests, so to move things along quickly, you have to ask big. You have to ask unreasonably.

Think of what would make your requests unreasonable. Whatever you were going to ask for, ask for more. Whenever you wanted it, ask for it sooner. Whatever you were willing to pay or trade, ask for it for less, or free. You get the idea.

Make your requests for more. Bigger. Faster. Cheaper. Outrageouser.

Make them unreasonable.

Turning reasonable requests into unreasonable ones:

Once you've begun the practice of making requests, you can quickly step up to the practice of making unreasonable ones.

A good place to start is with something you were going to ask for already.

Take any request you were going to make, and amplify it. Ask for more than you had originally considered. Much more. Ask for it sooner. Much sooner. If you were making one request of someone, make a second—or a third.

Just to get in the groove, take five requests you had planned to make, and be unreasonable in what you ask for.
If you like, keep a list to track your requests.

Reasonable request	Unreasonable request	Date asked

I've just asked you to be unreasonable—and you're going to do it, aren't you?

See? It works!

WHY SHOULD I DO THAT? **37**

There's that nasty word again—"Why?"

You can have the biggest vision in the world, but without people taking action, all you have is a pretty picture. No results.

Enrollment is the bridge between what you envision and getting a commitment from other people to take action.

When you communicate a possible future of such compelling power that people around you see themselves in that future and begin to take action, that's enrollment. Your ability to cause others to stand in your vision and act is key to your success.

If people work for you, or report to you somehow, you can tell them what to do. It sounds like too much trouble. Why bother with enrollment?

Because there is a great jump in what people are actually willing to do, how far they are willing to go, to accomplish an end to which they have bought in.

Sounds hard, doesn't it?

What if I gave you a formula for enrolling people?

Five Steps of Enrollment

1. Establish a foundation for relationship.

This is the easiest step, but one many people skip. Talk to people as if they are someone you care about. Discover things in common. Get under their skin a little bit. Show them some of what's under your skin.

2. Have a conversation about the possibilities of your venture.

Share what you see as the possibilities of your venture. Using that as a background, find out what is needed and wanted by them. What are they trying to have happen in their own lives, or their own ventures? Is there a match of some kind? Do your possibilities mesh? Where is the overlap? Is there something shared?

3. What's in it for them?

Why should people help you?

Discuss what specific opportunities exist in your business for them. How can participating in your enterprise help them get what they need or want? How can your project provide that?

What is the particular role you would like them to fill—and how can that role deliver what they want?

4. Discuss/suggest/invent possible specific actions by which they can realize the opportunity and the possibility you just discussed.

Make requests for them to move on those actions, with deliverables and due dates. Have them make promises. Record the commitments.

5. Talk about what you might do if things don't work out as planned.

What are the alternatives, what's the fallback position? What actions should you and they take to keep things on track?

Notice that nowhere in this entire conversation is there any discussion about what you want. Keep it that way.

This is not about you.

It is about the possibilities of your venture, and the possibilities for others, and how those two come together and get into action.

And that's it.

Never complain never explain.   U.S. Marines

There's a myth that things happen for a reason. The facts don't support this.

Things just happen. You've seen the bumper sticker. Things happen. Period. They either happen the way you want or some other way.

Either the job got done or it didn't. The result got produced or it didn't. Something else might have been produced instead of the result you wanted—and you may want to keep track of what—but with respect to your expectations, either you met them or you did not.

Now, what about why?

Of course why something occurred the way it did is important. If you lacked manpower, or materials, or money, or time, you'd want to know those things. You'd want to be able to provide whatever is missing so that your objectives can be reached.

But people like reasons (read: excuses) because they let them duck the responsibility. When you say, "It didn't happen because…" you are saying that whatever follows "because" is a reason, and the reason caused whatever result you are trying to dodge responsibility for.

"Whys" and "becauses" are descriptions of circumstances, as if circumstances made a difference. And you know what George Bernard Shaw said about circumstances.

"People are always blaming their circumstances for what they are. I don't believe in circumstances. The people who get on in this world are the people who get up and look for the circumstances they want, and if they can't find them, make them."

To cause quantum leap growth in your venture, you have to be completely responsible for the outcome. When you are responsible there are no whys or becauses. There is the outcome, or there is not the outcome.

Here's a great way to save time and get more done:

Stop making excuses.

___

Don't offer explanations when things don't go as planned, and don't listen to them from others. This produces a very black and white view of things—promised results on one hand and reasons, explanations, and excuses on the other.

This achieves three useful things. One, it forces you to look squarely at your results, and acknowledge what you actually accomplished.

Two, it holds you clearly responsible for the results you did produce.

Three, it saves everyone the time of having to listen to all the reasons why things didn't happen the way you'd hoped. For most people, not making excuses is a breakthrough all by itself. You've been doing it your whole life. And giving up reasons positions you for incredible change.

Say you don't meet a particular milestone on your timeline. Normally, you'd come up with some quite reasonable excuse as to why not. Instead, skip the excuse—don't spend any time on it at all—and start inventing new ways to get to your committed result.

This takes some getting used to—offering explanations is so ingrained. Just stop it. If you hear yourself making an excuse— stop yourself and say—"Oh. I didn't mean to say that. Now, what can we do to get on back on track?"

Sometimes you do want to know why a promised result wasn't produced. A new language is called for: When reporting on results, train yourself to speak in the following format:

"We said we would accomplish _____."

"To do that we would do _____."

"What we actually did was _____."

"What we accomplished was _____."

"What was missing was _____."

"What we need to do next is _____."

Not only will you get more done, you'll have a much more clear picture of what's really happening inside your organization.

39

Are your people all pulling in the same direction?

Have you ever been part of a group or team where everyone has an opinion? (Have you ever not been?) Suppose each member has something different to say about the vision. Everyone wants to personalize it, putting their own little spin on how things should look in the end.

Sound familiar?

It's human nature, and as a leader, it can work for you. The more each member invests in the final formulation—the more they call it their own—the more they fight for its realization. But with all these different opinions, how are you going to have a unified vision, one you can all jointly realize?

Chunk up. All conflict is ultimately a matter of details. Move the conversation up to a higher level of abstraction. At some point, all points of view coalesce into agreement. Whatever that level is, that's the level at which you need to hold the vision.

Don't get so abstract that the shared vision becomes a generality without any meaning. A powerful vision is visceral, people feel it in a way that gives them goose bumps.

You will lose feeling if you get too abstract. The vision then is worthless.

Another approach is to resolve conflicts through creative alignment. People generally object to just a part, not the whole. What part needs to change so everyone can "buy in?"

Can the rest of the group let go of a particular nuance so everyone is included? Keep tweaking the language until everyone is enrolled.

Once reached, this degree of agreement is very motivating. You've truly forged a shared vision—lots of energy gets released— a cheer may go up in the room. You'll know you've got something powerful to work with.

Try this, and watch your conflicts go away.

40 *KEEPING YOUR WORD*

Do what you say you'll do.

Keeping your word is the simplest way to keep things moving fast and cause breakthroughs. Think about it: if you always do what you say, and you say you are creating breakthroughs, then you will create breakthroughs.

Is it really that simple? Yes—it really is. Make commitments. Big ones. Do everything you said, when you said you would.

The problem is that many of us are just not good at doing what we say when we say, to the specifications we promise. We do some of the things, perhaps late, and with partial results.

Not nearly good enough.

First, resolve to keep your word. Make the promise to yourself that you are going to do whatever you must to honor the commitments you make. Next, declare that your word is good. "I keep my promises."

Last, only make promises you plan to keep.

Start small. What if you usually come late to meetings. One way to raise the tone of your venture is to start showing up early.

Would that have an impact?

Of course it would. Make a new promise to yourself—and you tell everyone around you—"I will be on time from now on." Then do everything to insure you are early for every meeting. Not just the important ones—every one.

Perhaps you don't return phone calls. Or you don't ship orders. Or you don't pick up the groceries on the way home.

Whatever practice you pick, start keeping your word in the small things. When you get good at showing up early, expand can your level of commitments. Make larger and larger promises, and make sure you deliver.

At some point, you will simply trust yourself. You will know that when you say you are going to do something, you can consider it done.

What power! What creative ability!
No matter what you say is going to happen, it will.

That's a breakthrough!

Do this:

Pick an area where you regularly do not keep your word.

Make a public declaration that from now on, you will do the thing you do not currently do, when you say, and how you say. Like showing up on time, that sort of thing.

Now go off and do it for a while.
When you get very good at showing up on time, raise the stakes. What is something more important that you would like to declare?

When you always do what you say, people notice. You become someone they can count on.
That opens important doors to your future.

---

41 *BROKEN PROMISES*

The best laid plans o' mice an' men gang aft aglee.

Robert Burns, perhaps

Or, to use a more colloquial expression: *No matter how hard you try, stuff happens.*

A promise is a declaration that you will do something, perhaps by a certain date, and maybe including specifics of how it will be done.

Making a promise is giving your word. If you have trained yourself and you are in the habit of keeping your word, making promises is a powerful way to get things done. How? You make a promise, then you deliver the goods. The bigger the promise, the more goods you deliver. Want to deliver bigger goods? Make bigger promises.

There's a catch, however. Sometimes you don't deliver the goods.

Sometimes you run out of time, or you can't manage the resources, or you get too busy, or you just plain forget. In other words, you've broken your promise.

There are now three things you can do. You can own up to not keeping your promise and make a new one.

You can try to justify not keeping your promise. Explain why you didn't and why that doesn't make you a bad person.

Or you can do what many people do—weasel your way out and hope no one notices. I recommend the first option. It's clean and neat. It has loads of integrity.

Fear of breaking promises is what keeps people from making

them in the first place. This fear gums up the works and prevents the kind of accelerated change your business needs. A breakthrough business is fueled by big requests and big promises. So all you can do is make those big promises, and come clean if you break them.

Do this:

List five (or maybe ten) promises you've broken in the recent past and which are sitting there smelling like spoiled milk. Include whom you made the promise to, and check it off when you have acknowledged the broken promise, and cleaned it up.

You'll be amazed at how good that feels. For both parties.

Raise your sights.

By now you've experienced the 1-5 scale or the 1-10 scale. Maybe you've even taken a self-test in this book graded that way. 1-10 is a good way to gauge where you think you are versus where you think you should be. It's a scale relative to your expectations.

Let's take one right now.

On a scale of 1-10, where 1 is low and 10 is high, where do you stand with respect to moving faster than the speed of change? Write your answer below and date it. Every so often, come back to the page and rate yourself again.

Rating   Date

Your number means you have produced some result on a scale where your highest expectations are 10. Now recalibrate. Take whatever rating you've given yourself, and call it a 1.

Whoa!

Take a deep breath. We've just completely changed the game.

Play along even if you don't like it. If you were at 7 or a 9, and now you are at 1, that means you have to redefine 10, doesn't it?

So what is a 10? Pause a moment and think this through.

Write below the things that would define a 10.

Reaching 10 would be a full-scale breakthrough, wouldn't it?

How are you going to make your venture a 10 on the breakthrough scale? From where you are now, how are you going to get there? What are you going to do next?

That is your next step. Design a game plan to realize what you've described on the list above.

As you define the steps needed, you may be surprised to find that it's not as hard as you thought.

43 *NEVER GIVE 'EM ANSWERS*

The wise man doesn't give the right answers, he poses the right questions.

Claude Levi-Strauss

Want the best management advice ever?

Ask great questions.

Great questions help your venture three ways. The quality of the questions you ask determines the quality of your information. The quality of those same questions influences the way people in your project act. Perhaps most importantly, the questions you ask govern absolutely what you think about.

Use Rudyard Kipling's six honest serving men: who, what, where, why, how and when, but use each in each in the right context. For instance, why questions often elicit excuses or justifications. With a broken promise, ask when instead. When will it be made good.

When something doesn't work, ask what can we do, or how can we make it work. If something needs to be done, ask who will do it, and when, and maybe how.

Make sure you ask questions which define the information or ideas you are after. Ask general questions when you want a broad response and specific to focus thinking narrowly. Frame your questions carefully.

Ask "How can we...?" instead of "Is this possible?" Ask questions designed to generate answers which will rocket your venture forward. Ask your people: "How can we create a really major breakthrough?"

Ask "What will bring customer X to the table?" to build a strategy for customer X. Ask "How can we serve ten times the customers?" to figure out how to serve ten times the customers.

Frame your questions to create the result you want.

Don't worry about the answers unless you don't get any. Instead, worry about the questions.

Great questions.

How do you create great questions?

Glad you asked. *(That was a good one right there!)*

Start with a blank page, or better yet, a large whiteboard. Write at the top a problem whose solution would be a breakthrough. Then write ten great questions, the answers to which will transform your venture.

My "breakthrough problem" is _____.

10 great questions are:

1. _____?
2. _____?
3. _____?
4. _____?
5. _____?
6. _____?
7. _____?
8. _____?
9. _____?
10. _____?

Look at each of these. Would the answer to the question bring you the results you're after?

If so, great question.

44

Do you listen when you talk to yourself?

Every venture has a way of talking about itself. Even when the conversation is "positive," it typically acts as a limit on the success of the venture.

Your conversations define the way you think of things. They define who you see as your customer base and what you think is your product. They circumscribe the actions you take, the way you are organized, how you view yourselves in the world.

They determine your outcomes.

Once you become aware that there is a conversation, it can be changed. The first thing is to notice it. What do you habitually say about yourselves and the environment in which you function? Become aware of how that conversation influences the choices you make.

One option is simply to not get locked into any particular conversation at all. Train yourself to notice that you are saying things repeatedly in a particular way. Stop every time you notice it, suggesting something new and fresh instead.

In that moment, ask yourself what would be a way to speak about this which would add power to the situation? What new conversation might open up new possibilities?

What are some of the things you habitually say about your venture?

What are some things you might say instead?

V

FAST DIRECTION

One of the possible pitfalls of higher performance is going faster in the wrong direction. First locate your navigational star—then propel yourself in the right direction.

WHAT'S POSSIBLE? **45**

Reach for the outer limits. Stretch.

Build your business upon your idea of what is possible, not what is likely or reasonable. Reasonable propositions produce reasonable, predictable results. They are the things you think will come to pass, that make sense according to what has been done before. They are comfortably within the bounds of what you have produced in the past.

There is nothing wrong with reasonable ideas, they just never produce extraordinary results.

So, what is possible? Anything you can think of.

In fact, a thing becomes possible simply because you can think it. By declaring something possible, it takes on an existence it didn't have until that moment. Just because you said so, you transform the impossible into the possible.

This gives you, the entrepreneur, the captain of your own life, tremendous power.

There is no proof required for these declarations of possibility. When you declare something is possible you need not know the route to its accomplishment. Declaration of possibility is the first step. Until you call something possible, you are unable to take action on it.

Decide what you intend to accomplish—and say—*"I declare such-and-such is possible."*

By recognizing possibilities, you open yourself up to seeing things you would never have seen before.

It's a beautiful view.

46 BURY THE PAST

Completion allows you to put the past where it belongs—in the past.

When complete you are free to move forward without dragging the past with you. You leave behind all the recriminations, regrets and hand wringing. There is no finger pointing or guilt. There is no trying to *"do it right this time."* No *"shoulda, woulda, coulda."*

You are complete when there is nothing more to be said about what has taken place. It has all been put to bed; what is left is simply doing what is next to do.

Completion gives your venture an air of lightness and freshness. It's required for your business to move past the speed of change. It frees you from fixating on the past, from doing more of what you've already done.

The process of completion gives you a chance to look at what has transpired, in an impersonal way, and capture whatever knowledge is available.

Completion, giving you the blank slate to perform fresh actions, transforms reaction into creation.

Completion Questions

These questions will help you be complete with your venture's past.

What were your objectives?

What results did you accomplish?

What unintended results did you produce?

What worked?

What didn't work?

What was missing (resources, skills, knowledge, attitudes, relationships) which would have enabled you to deliver more completely?

What's next?

What else needs to be said?

47

FIRST THINGS...

There is a fundamental, but difficult to accept truth about the nature of things:

Some important things are more important than other important things.

No, the above sentence does not have a typo. Even among the things you call important there is an order and a ranking. The word priority is derived from the Latin word primus, meaning first. Priorities are the things that are first.

Everything else comes after.

To move forward faster, you need clearly established priorities. Which things come first? Which things are going to make the biggest difference, create the most value? Where will you get the greatest leverage? Do sales come first? Do existing customers come first? Does conception or design come first? Do your stakeholders come first? Does your health come first? Does your karma come first?

You have to decide what comes first, then second, and so on. The things that come first are your priorities. Things that are second are not priorities, at least not at this moment. When all the first things are settled and put to bed, then, maybe, will these second things become first things. Unless there are new, more important things which arise.

You see, your priorities are not static—they require continual reexamination—to know which things are now first.

This ordered list, your priorities, governs how your energies and resources are best spent. Spend your resources on things which come first, and your venture will flourish. Spend your resources on things that come second or third, and your venture may still flourish—but less. Or it will suffer.

One fact you may have to come to grips with is that things which are not first priorities may never get accomplished. This is OK, as long as you've selected your priorities properly.

How do you select priorities?

Step 1.

Ignore for the moment all the things you think you have to do which are not important.

Right off the hop these unimportant things are not priorities. To consider whether something is important, reference it against your list of goals. If an action, or a department, or any sort of "thing" gives you leverage (low input, high output) in moving towards your goals, it is probably important.

Split a blank page down the middle. On the left, list all the items you consider to be important.

Step 2.

Sort the left-hand list to create the ordered priorities.

Compare each item to every item below it on the list. If one is more important, keep comparing that item. When done, put the most important one on the right-hand list, and cross it off the left hand list. Take the next available item on the left hand list and start again.

The sorted right hand list are your priorities. Do they feel right? Do they pass the "reasonableness test?" If you concentrate your energies and resources on the items on this list, in order, are you likely to turn your business into a runaway success? This list should contain only items of "first importance."

Strike anything that doesn't fit that description, and sort again.

48

SACRIFICE

Someone once said that "Ordered priorities are the wellspring of discipline." Discipline is a scary word, for some. Implied in the notion of priorities is another word that scares a lot of people:

SACRIFICE

Sacrifice means giving up something important for something even more important. It is not a sacrifice to give up something you do not care about. For many people, this concept is both obvious and a bit frightening.

In a world of boundless resources, there is no need for sacrifice. Most enterprises, however much we like to talk about abundance, exist in resource-constrained environments. In a world of limited resources prioritizing and sacrifice are inextricably bound.

Because you can accomplish only so much with the available resources in any particular time frame, the tasks of each day, the schedule of each week, every decision at all—must be considered in terms of its ultimate value to your enterprise—now and in the future.

Concentrate your energies and resources on the elements that will have the greatest effect. This implies that some things—however much you love them, however much you are excited about them—may have to be sacrificed for the sake of other things having even greater impact.

You've done the groundwork by setting up your list of priorities.

Take your to-do lists, your project lists, your hiring lists, all your lists, and compare them to your list of high priorities. Does an item strongly advance your topmost priorities? Work on it now. Lavish it with resources and time until complete.

Does it fall towards to bottom of the list?

You know what to do with that one.

49

To practice meditation, bring all your attention to a single point of reference—your breathing, a mantra, a spot on the wall—and direct all your energy towards that point.

Outrageous success requires the same single-pointed focus. Choose your most important undertaking. Decide to eliminate all other undertakings which might compete for your attention. Clear your mind of all distractions.

Focus is concentrating all your time, energy, and resources on a single important object of your attention. Spending them on anything else diminishes your chances for success. Sometimes critically.

Think about where your attention wanders during the course of a day. How much more effective would you be if all your energy was used single-pointedly? Decide what is important and on what you are going to concentrate. Then work on that, nothing else.

Anything else will diminish your success.

Do this:

Gather together your purpose, vision, mission and goals. Review these to ensure they are aligned, and you are aligned with them. Decide to pursue that direction.

Consider your resource commitments—are they all in service to this direction? Gracefully extricate yourself from those commitments which are not.

Examine all your projects and initiatives. Are they in service to this direction? Ruthlessly cancel those which are not.

Picture yourself as a straight-shafted arrow, speeding towards the small circle in the center of a target. Nothing distracts that arrow. It has only one place to go.

That's focus.

50   *AIMING YOUR BOW*

What direction are you headed in?

Can you say it out loud, without hesitation, letting everyone around you know what path you are on?

Imagine filling your car with gas, turning the ignition key, putting it in gear, getting on the freeway, and pressing the pedal-to-the-metal. Full speed ahead. Imagine that.

Wait—where are you headed?

You got on the road which goes south—is that what you had in mind? Surely it will take you somewhere, but is it where you wanted to go?

Say you did plan on South—toward your destination in that direction. Along the way you come upon a beautiful, tree-lined road—you take it.

Unfortunately it goes northwest. Whether this is a good idea depends on your drive's purpose. If this is a pleasure drive, you could be successful with any road that seemed pleasant. If your purpose is arriving at a certain destination at a certain time, you need clear directions, and the discipline to stay on the path.

Direction is not complicated.

You determine your direction based on your purpose, mission and vision. Your direction is towards your goals. State out loud and on paper where you are going, what you intend to accomplish. Take a compass bearing in that direction and proceed. Focus on that direction, and don't be diverted by all the pretty opportunities that arise along the way.

Remember: Arrows don't turn in mid-flight.

INVENTING THE FUTURE **51**

The future is whatever you say it's going to be.

How could it be otherwise? The future is a mental construct, it does not exist in the material world. The only thing it could be is something we say.

Leaders are, by definition, people who take a stand—they say what's possible in the future, and further declare that what they say is possible is going to happen.

People tend to act on whatever future they believe is possible, which makes leadership a highly reliable, self-fulfilling, positive feedback system.

The questions then are what is possible, and what is the future? When most people ask what is possible, they really are considering what's probable. When most people consider the future, they actually think of some variation on their past. The past—only better. The past—only much better. The past—only worse. You get the picture.

The future for most people is generally a continuation of the past.

Another type of future is simply invented. It might be a continuation of the past, but not necessarily. It might be a complete break with anything that has ever happened before. From the standpoint of the present, this type of break-with-the-past future is every bit as valid as the "past plus ten-per-cent" kind. After all, you can have whatever conversation you like, and if you can persuade people that this is a future worth having, you just might realize it.

So the future is whatever you are willing to make happen.

Leaders are people for whom the future exists as a source of inspiration. What will your future be?

52 *STRATEGY IS AN INVENTION—PART 1.*

Strategy is something you make up.

Strategy is what you will do as a company to realize your vision: what specifically will you accomplish, what meaning will your company have, and how will you create value and profits?

Don't ignore what you've done in the past—just don't be constrained by it. Don't ignore your marketplace, just don't fall into the trap of letting your competitors' actions define your own. And certainly don't ignore your customers—just don't think that your customers' wants and desires are the only measure of what you should seek to accomplish.

These references—past results, markets, competitors, customers, all must be taken into account—they create the context for your strategy.

But then, what it boils down to is: your strategy is the direction your venture will take, because you said so.

An invented strategy inspires you. It fulfills your vision for your company, and because you see how the realization of your strategy makes an important difference in the world, it inspires your team, your customers, and your prospects.

An invented strategy energizes all your constituents, where incrementalism just seems like more work. An invented strategy can propel your enterprise to greatness. An invented strategy can call forth achievements beyond what you currently consider possible. Breakthroughs and blockbusters are never founded on incremental improvement.

Invented strategies can change your company's relationship to the marketplace and to the world.

And like Athena from the forehead of Zeus, they spring from the minds of their inventors.

The route to creating strategy is simple—asking the right questions.

What direction can the company take now to realize your vision? What value proposition will you offer customers? What meaningful difference will you make in your marketplace? What meaningful difference will you make in your world? How do you want to affect the lives of your people, your customers, your clients? Your family?

Answer these questions and you are on road to inventing your strategy.

Here are some questions to help you formulate strategy.

What vision, purpose and values are embodied in your company? What would have them be realized even further?

What, specifically, would make your company "better" than it is now? *(More profitable, greater revenues, improved product, improved service, more value for the customer, etc.)*

If you could do absolutely anything in your industry, what would it be? Are you doing that now? If not, why not?

What are the most important reasons people buy your product or service? Why would you like people to buy your product? How do you rate on the 1-10 scale, with respect to those reasons? How could you improve that rating?

What are three major changes shaping your industry over the next five to ten years? In what ways are you positioned to participate in those changes?

What is the most important thing you have to offer your customers. Why is that important to you? Why is that important to your customers?

In your wildest fantasies, what do you want people to be able to say about your company, or your product? What is necessary for people to be able to say that?

What is happening in other industries that could be adapted to your business and your product offering?

What do you think is missing from your product offering? What would make your product really amazing!!!!?

What are your competitors doing that "blows your mind?" What are your competitors doing that "blows your customers' minds?" What should your competitors be doing that would "blow your mind?" Should you be doing that?

What have your customers told you they just can't get anywhere? Is that something you should offer?

What products are related to your current offering, that you could offer? What products do other companies (non-competitors) offer, which you could offer your customers? How would those products add value?

What actions could you take today which would double your profits in 24 months? How about in 12 months? What is missing for you to take those actions? What is in the way of you taking those actions?

What business are you really in? Should you pare down to just that business? Can you create additional value focused on that business only? What would make your product 10%—just 10%—better than anything in your market space?

What are the most glaring weaknesses of your company? What are you doing to redress them?

What is your vision for the next five years? Are you moving decisively towards realizing that vision? If not, what would move you in that direction? What are the key needs of the major stakeholders (owners, employees, customers, etc.)? Are those needs being served?

What are three things you'd really like to do—which would make a significant difference (to your customers, or perhaps, to the world)- but have excellent reasons for not doing? How valid are those excellent reasons?

What are the meaningful differences (the Gap) between your five-year vision for your company, and where you are now? What can you do to close the Gap that you are not doing now?

If you were starting from scratch, what would you do next?

What is the most dramatic trend that affects your industry? Are you part of that trend? Should you be?

What would you find truly meaningful?

54 *STRATEGY IS AN INVENTION—PART 2.*

Have you answered the strategic questions? If not, go back and answer them now.

OK, there are some more.

Are you building something totally new, or are you improving an existing idea?

What are the dimensions of the impact you want to have? Will it be faster? Better? Cheaper? Easier? Safer? More luxurious? More convenient? More portable? More entertaining? More universal?

From a high-level perspective, how will you marshal your resources and time your maneuvers to offer that value and make that difference?

Strategy is not evolutionary; it is revolutionary. Don't assume the old rules apply or let them guide your thinking. Breaking rules may actually be a way to conceive of strategy. Ask yourself, "What rules can we break?"

List three of them right here.

Old Rule #1

Old Rule #2

Old Rule #3

Consider which obsolete beliefs restrain growth in your company or your market. Make up your own assumptions. Test them first in your mind.

Einstein conceived of the "Theory of Relativity" using what he called a *gedanken* experiment. An experiment in the mind.

Old Belief #1

Old Belief #2

Old Belief #3

While you are considering Strategy, don't worry about whether you have the wherewithal to implement what you are thinking about.

If you do worry in this way, you are likely to compromise from the get-go. There will be plenty of room for compromise later, if you must. Ignore the resource constraints that dog you throughout the year. You will deal with these when the time comes. Author Gary Hamil offers his definition of strategy as the *"...quest to overcome resource constraints through a creative and unending pursuit of better resource leverage."*

You've answered a bunch of questions. You've cast out some old assumptions and beliefs and you are ready to bend or break some rules. Give it a try—articulate a strategy. What is the way you are going to bring your vision into reality?

Take a moment and write that down...

55

Give me a lever long enough and I can move the world.

Archimedes

Archimedes was talking about leverage—the physical principal that lets you to move a large mass with a limited amount of force. Leverage is getting more out than you put in.

In other words—low input, high output.

Leverage is critical to the success of your business. Think of it this way, if you invest ten dollars and get back eleven, you aren't getting rich very quickly, especially after you deduct for overhead. But if you invest ten dollars and get back one hundred...

Perhaps you intend to shift the opinions of a large group of individuals—talking to them one at a time may cause change one by one. But if you can craft a message to effectively reach them in a large group, you can affect many at one time; plus they interact, which can reinforce your message further. That's leverage.

If you can do it over the Internet—reaching thousands or even millions, at very little cost—that's really leverage.

Some things that provide leverage:

Strategic distribution partnerships multiply your sales efforts.

Borrowed money multiplies the effect of your invested capital.

Training multiplies the effectiveness of an employee.

Automated systems multiply the effects of your workforce.

Marketing multiplies the efforts of your sales force.

Mastermind groups multiply the effect of your intellect.

And leadership—the greatest source of people leverage, multiplies the efforts of your entire team.

How can you magnify the output from your inputs? What small changes can you make to get the greatest benefits from your valuable assets?

Look for ways to get ten out for every one in.

Some ways leverage can be created:

Creating incredible, over-the-top value for your customers.

Attracting great talent into your company.

Streamlining your sales process—the way customers buy your products.

Enhancing the distribution process—how you put your product into the hands of your customers.

Producing and delivering your product at low cost and high margins.

Promoting your business and gaining mind share among customers, investors, talent and industry influencers.

Strategic partnerships to make anything happen faster.

Optimizing how you use technology.

Taking care of your customers so well that they really feel taken care of.

Securing capital for investment in product, services and market development.

Anticipating the future and doing something about it now.

Sharing a powerful context—vision, purpose, values and mission—which inspires your stakeholders, and keeps everyone doing their part at a very high level of performance.

How else is leverage gained in your business? What specific areas will transform your venture into a high-performance powerhouse?

Do this:

Identify three areas where you need to increase your leverage.

1.
2.
3.

Now list one way to increase your leverage in each area.

For each of these high leverage areas:

- Establish performance measures and goals.

- Set the baseline: what is your current level of performance against these measures?

- What strategies and tactics are currently planned or being implemented?

- What resources are currently allocated? Is that sufficient or do you want to make changes?

- What new strategies and tactics do you want to implement in these areas?

- What will make this area better? What will make it go faster?

- What would create a breakthrough?

- Now, how are you going to make it happen?

KEEPING YOUR BALANCE **56**

Piloting a successful company is like walking a tightrope... You've got to keep your balance or you might hurt yourself.

Keeping your balance is a personal thing; the list of things to balance is unique to each of us.

What is balance? Balance is making sure that each of the elements in your business and in your life is getting the attention it deserves. One of the keys is prioritizing—putting the most attention on the things that make the most difference.

One could easily conclude that everything else should get ignored or sidelined in the process. That would be a serious mistake.

The principal of balance says something else. Short-term concerns must be balanced by long term ones. Production capability needs are balanced by sales and marketing needs. Work life is balanced by family life. Corporate health is balanced by personal health.

Each element of these pairs of "opposites" is required to sustain the other. If you give all your attention to production and none to sales, your company will have plenty of product but no customers. If you focus on the short term without considering the long term, you are likely make some disastrous decisions. If you put all your attention on work and none on your family, your relationships will suffer.

Sacrifice production capability for sales or vice versa, and you will always be playing catch up. Sacrifice your home life for work and you may never be able to catch up. To keep things going over the long haul, you've got to divide your attention amongst the critical opposites.

57   *SUSTAINABILITY REQUIRES BALANCE*

How do you reconcile the principal of balance with the concept of priorities? Figure out what your current priorities are and spend most of your time on those.

Leave time in your schedule for the balancing things. A little well-thought-out attention paid can save you lots of repair work later on.

> Do this: List each critical area in your (life, business, etc.) and its balancing partner. Consider whether you are short-changing one or the other.
>
> _____ balanced by _____
> _____ balanced by _____
> _____ balanced by _____
> _____ balanced by _____
> _____ balanced by _____
> _____ balanced by _____
> _____ balanced by _____
> _____ balanced by _____

Highlight the areas where you're out of balance. Then do something about it.

CRITICAL SUCCESS FACTORS 58

What are your critical success factors?

Every venture has a set of factors critical to its success. For instance, sales, production, customer service, people and finance, are critical to the generic company. If you fail in any area on the list, your venture will suffer—badly. To have a breakthrough in business, someone must understand each.

And master it.

Step one

Identify the factors critical to the success of your venture.

On the next page is a general list for almost any business. It may be appropriate for yours. More likely, it will require a bit of tinkering.

What functional issues will bring your venture truly outlandish returns? If you were to increase your effectiveness or performance in a specific area, what would it mean for your company? If you were to suffer a setback in a particular department, what would be the implications?

Can your business flourish if you stop paying attention to any of these factors?

- ◙ Revenue and/or profit growth

- ◙ Product development

- ◙ Customer satisfaction

- ◙ Productivity

- ◙ Product quality

- ◙ Strategic relationships

- ◙ New customer growth

     Personnel attraction and retention

- ◙ Financing

- ◙ Positioning

- ◙ Market penetration

- ◙ _____

- ◙ _____

- ◙ _____

- ◙ _____

- ◙ _____

Cross out factors which are not critical, and add ones you think are.

Step two

Devise a system of measurement and a set of objectives for each of the factors. Create a baseline measure to mark your progress.

Step three

Invent and implement a series of initiatives designed to impact those measures to achieve your objectives.

You can use this list of critical factors to keep your business in balance. Draw a "radar chart" with equal wedges for all the factors. Mark each axis (each critical factor) with the objective values for its own measurements. Plot along the axis showing how far you've gotten in achieving your objectives. This chart will show clearly whether things are in proper balance.

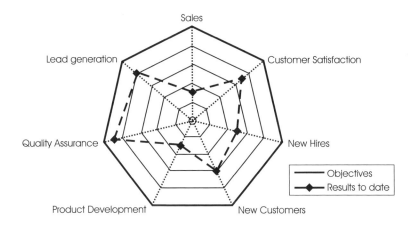

Create a list of factors and a "radar chart" for every project you take on.

When you find an imbalance, fix it immediately. Don't let your business run the road with a flat!

Begin at the ending, go to the beginning, and then stop.

In the court of King Arthur, there was a wizard named Merlin whose job it was to foretell the Kingdom's future. Merlin could do this because of what you might call a special situation.

Born an old man, Merlin grew younger every day. His life was going backwards and, for Merlin, what King Arthur thought was the future had already happened. Relative to Arthur's, Merlin's whole life was a déjà vu—he merely reported what he had already seen in his youth.

Merlin can be a great inspiration when you construct plans for things you don't know how to do. If you are playing the breakthrough game, you often commit to things you have no idea how to accomplish. That's one of the essential keys. You put your big foot in your mouth, and say "Yes. We'll do that..."

Even if you have no idea how.

Not a problem. Following Merlin, you mentally place yourself in the future. Imagine yourself standing at the end of a long time line—you have already achieved your specific goal.

Imagine or visualize—how did you do it? What actions did you take? What resources did you secure? What skills did you develop? Who's help did you enlist?

Ask these questions in a stepwise fashion starting from the end. Just before you reached your goal, what was the last significant thing you did? You would know what had to happen immediately before success, wouldn't you? What actions, what resources, what skills, whose help? Of course you would. Put those things on the timeline with a date. That is your last intermediate milestone.

Again ask yourself, immediately before reaching that last milestone, what did you do? Mark that on the timeline. And just before that milestone... And so on, moving closer and closer in time, right up until the present.

Each significant result has a key action that would have to precede it, and each key action a significant result that would have to proceed it. And so you build your plan one step at a time, backwards, from the future to now.

Lastly, perform a reality check. Think it all through forwards. If you add the necessary resources, skills, and knowledge, take each action in turn, and reach each milestone, is that likely to produce the results you intend to produce?

Breakthrough tip: Don't limit your use of the Merlin Method to times when you find yourself clueless. Let Merlin help your unconscious mind develop alternate strategies, and compare their effectiveness to the way you already knew.

Don't be afraid to be backward.

60 *WISDOM FROM THE (S)AGES*

This little poem says more about leadership than much of the existing professional literature. I cloak myself in its judgment, and wish I could master its elegance.

Go to the people
Learn from them
Honor them
Start with what they know
Build on what they have
But of a good leader
Who talks little
When the work is done,
When his aim fulfilled,
The people will say
'We did this ourselves.'

Lao Tzu

Time management is a myth.

To get an idea of just how silly it is, you have to realize that the very concept of time was invented by people who didn't have enough of it. When pre-historic man needed more food, he said to his cave mates, "Let's go get food." When they had bagged a saber tooth or a wooly mammoth, they came home. Simple.

As life became somewhat more complicated, people started to say things like, "Meet me at the second tree by the river at day-break." As transactions among men increased in frequency and complexity, that system too became inadequate. There were too many appointments to keep so time was invented to manage all the goings on. And right after that came the world's most overused phrase:

"I don't have enough time."

What is the answer to this age-old cry?

You can't manage time. You can only choose what you do with it.

This may seem trivial and obvious—I assure you it is not; I know that because of the sheer numbers of people who haven't done it. Figure out what is really important right now, and do those things. And only those things.

Think about it. You have a limited amount of time each day, week, and so on. You can use that time for things that matter and make a difference, or you can fill it up with trivia. That's a very basic choice.

You already know what is important—things which will make a significant difference to your business, in the short term and the long term. The squeaky wheel theory has to go.

You don't have to answer the phone just because it's ringing. You don't have to respond just because you've received an email. You don't have to have a conversation now just because someone enters your office. Do what matters.

Skip or delegate everything else.

Attend to your priorities. Everything else can slide. If you spent your entire day working on the most important thing on your plate, would that have been a day well spent? Even if you didn't complete the task? Of course it would.

On the other hand, if you squandered the day on unimportant squeaky wheels, that would be a wasted day.

Use the prioritizing system described elsewhere in this book to organize what is important to your venture and what is not.

The breakthrough comes in spending your time on only those things.

Time Management Priority Style.

▣ For each day, make a list of three to six high priority items you intend to accomplish that day. Do this at the close of the previous work day, or the beginning of this one.

▣ Work on the first item until it is complete. If it isn't complete at the end of the day, keep working the next day until it is.

▣ When that item is complete, review your list to see if it is still appropriate. Recreate it if necessary.

▣ If two things have equal priority and you have no tie-breakers, simply choose one, or apportion your time—4 hours for one, 4 hours for the other. Use any arbitrary system, but only work on those two things until complete.

▣ No matter what, only work on those things that are most important to your success.

Charles Schwab, the visionary who created U.S. Steel early in the 20th century, paid a management consultant twenty-five thousand 1920s dollars for this little system.

Use it well. He did.

Want a breakthrough in how you use your time?

Find out where you currently spend it! If you've never tracked how you spend your time, you may be in for a surprise.

There are a few ways to do this. One is to note the time at a the beginning of each task, and at the end, logging the difference. The hard part of this system is handling interruptions. You might start working on a report at 10:15 and finish at 3:30. That's 5-1/4 hours, except that you spent 45 minutes at lunch and took a bunch of phone calls.

Another way is to write down what you've been doing for the past 15 minutes, every quarter hour. I prefer this method. It makes it easier to account for "interruptions", lunch or multitasking.

Some people like to track this on their computer. Unless you have a pocket computer or PDA, I suggest you use pen and paper. It's much more portable. Get a stack of 3x5 index cards or a spiral pocket notepad.

Start a fresh page for every day, and make a new entry every 15 minutes.

Do this for at least two weeks, or longer if you can stand it. No matter how long you go, you will learn a lot. When you are done, summarize where your time has gone.

You may be shocked, but you'll know where you stand.

Now that you have a baseline, you can make some management decisions. You may find you are spending way too much time on correspondence—voice mail, emails, etc. Perhaps you are in too many long meetings. Or your travel time to clients is unreasonably long. Or whatever.

The possible problems are far too numerous to list, but each problem presents an opportunity for streamlining your operation and creating a breakthrough in time and productivity.

Have everyone in your talent pool do this. Trim the time wasters.

63   *PARETO'S MAGIC FORMULA*

Back in the 19th century, one Vilfredo Pareto, an Italian economist, quantified the general relationship between a minority of producers and a majority of output.

Sound familiar? The Pareto Principle (the 80/20 rule) says that in most cases, 80% of production comes from 20% of producers. Quality guru J.M. Juran referred to Pareto's Principal as "the Vital Few and the Trivial Many."

The 80/20 rule has powerful implications for every area of your business. You can create a breakthrough in almost any area of your business by applying this simple concept. 20% of your effort will generate 80% of your results. Also, 20% of your results absorb 80% of your resources or efforts.

The trick is knowing which is the right 20%—distinguishing the Vital Few from the Trivial Many.

20% of your customers yield 80% or your revenues, and 20% of your customers yield 80% of your profit. There is also a top 20% of customer types, a top 20% of territories, and a top 20% of distributors. Which customers get the most service? Your service team spends 80% of its time on 20% of the customers—although they may not be the most profitable 20%.

All prospects are not created equal. 20% of your prospects have the potential for 80% of your future profits. Are your salespeople spending their time proportionately? Have them do an opportunity analysis to highlight the Vital Few.

Salesperson productivity also fits the 80/20 rule. 20% of your sales force produces 80% of your sales. Should you lavish equal resources on all your salespeople?

Invent ways to take your 20% and make them even more effective. An assistant or a dedicated account team could be concentrated around your top performers to increase their productivity even more.

If you have multiple products, services, geographies, customer tiers, etc., 80% of your profits will be come from 20% of the segments. Fully allocate your costs and rank your segments in profit order. Consider dropping, selling or trading less profitable ones.

What about the rest of your people? 80% of the useful work in your company is done by 20% of your staff. Guaranteed. Once again, you should figure out who's getting what done, and improve (or remove) the rest.

80/20 works wonders for time management. Odds are, 80% of your time is spent on Trivial Many activities. Do the 80/20 analysis and discover which executive activities produce the most value for your company. Refocus your time and place your attention on the Vital Few. Delegate the Trivial Many, or drop them altogether.

Are you getting the hang of this?

80/20 analysis can be applied to every aspect of your company. Look for things with multiple inputs and multiple outputs. We've touched on sales, marketing, quality, compensation and executive effectiveness. How else could 80/20 help you produce extraordinary results?

Do this process in a spreadsheet program where you can sort and re-sort the table.

Step 1

Segment whatever it is you are trying to analyze.

Generally, the segments suggest themselves. Salespeople are already segmented by name. Market segments include product type, product line, geography, demographics, price points and customer size. A consulting company might segment by {large customers—long engagements, large customers—short engagements, etc.}. Alternatively, {service contracts, management consulting, training, white papers, research}.

You get the idea.

Step 2

Create a spreadsheet similar to the example below, which lists your segments by name (or number), along with the characteristics you are analyzing. For instance, you can compare sales versus margin, or sales versus total profits (example below), or output to number of defective products.

One very telling analysis is hours spent vs. profit generated.

Once you create the spreadsheet, sort it in order of most important characteristics. Many companies use revenue as their defining criteria, but, when they consider it, are really more interested in profits. (But only when they consider it.)

Sort or rank them by productivity. Set it up with a few different ways to rank things—in this example, sales and profits. You might want to add other columns to get more information out of this exercise. Salespeople can be ranked by total sales volume and marginal profits. Customer segments can be ranked the same way, or by sales volume and total profitability.

If you were responsible for sales in the above organization, where would you be spending your time and your resources?

This type of simple analysis is often overlooked. But the results can run counter to our assumptions about what's productive and what isn't.

How often have you stressed the obvious instead of the truly productive?

Do the math. Then make the changes.

Sorted by Sales		
Segment	% Sales for Segment	% Profits for Segment
Red	24	37
Blue	16	16
Yellow	15	-4
Green	12	35
Purple	9.1	-12
White	8	11
Brown	8	21
Black	7.9	-4

Sorted by Profits		
Segment	% Sales for Segment	% Profits for Segment
Red	24	37
Blue	12	35
Yellow	8	21
Green	16	16
Purple	8	11
White	15	-4
Brown	7.9	-4
Black	9.1	-12

64   *IT'LL NEVER BE PERFECT*

Perfection is impossible. Get used to it.

Perfection is what happens when you get everything exactly right. All the pieces fit together in the best way conceivable. There are no defects, flaws or blemishes of any kind. Nothing is lacking and your outcome is completely suited to the situation.

Excellence, on the other hand, refers to something superior; of the highest value, the finest quality, and exceptional goodness.

The quest for perfection is an empty pursuit—an often fruitless and frustrating game of the ego. The costs of perfection are often well out of proportion to the benefits, and perfection's striving is likely to cost you profits and customers.

The pursuit of excellence—superior value, fine quality, exceptional goodness—is likely to yield big rewards in terms of customers and profits.

Perfection leads you into problems. Perfectionists are only happy when "nothing at all is ever wrong", and are continually unhappy. Something, no matter how small or insignificant, is always—well, wrong.

Excellence leads you to breakthroughs. Not seeking something perfect—without blemish or flaw—but doing something great— providing great value, great quality.

Don't you need perfection for great quality? In mission critical, real time systems, yes. In systems where lives are at stake, yes.

But wait... people say *"we couldn't tolerate defects in medicine."*

Yet they happen all the time. What about airlines—we need zero defects there, don't we? Again, scheduling, overbooking, meals issues, even grounded flights. These are all defects.

Would the benefits of eliminating these defects outweigh the costs? In both of these cases it is excellence we want. Excellent diagnosis and treatment. Excellent takeoffs and landings.

Examine the costs and the benefits of perfection. What would zero defects in all areas cost you and what would it yield to you and to your customers? Isn't it really excellence you are after?

Excellence is possible. Commit to it.

VI

FAST ACTION

In the end, it really comes down to what you do.

ACTION 65

The essence of action is accomplishment.   Martin Heidegger

Ultimately, the only thing that produces results is action. Only those tasks on which you act get done. Nothing else.

> *Wishing does not produce results.*
> *Having good intentions does not produce results.*
> *Neither objectives nor goals produce results.*
> *Plans do not produce results.*
> *Affirmations do not produce results.*
> *Zen does not produce results.*
> *Wanting something, even really badly, does not produce results.*
> *Being a good person does not produce results.*

The only thing that produces results is taking action, and not stopping until the thing is done.

Many people find this a little harsh, and try to find evidence that wishing, prayer, good intentions, objectives, goals or affirmations got something done.

If that is your reaction, ask yourself the following question:

How may times have I (wished, intended, etc., etc.,) and gotten something accomplished?

Is it 100% of the time? 80%? 50%? 2%?

You may be forced to admit that those "not-action" things— wishing, intending and planning—do not actually accomplish the results, and only doing—specifically, taking action—gets things done.

Everything else is coincidence, wishful thinking or careless observation.

Now this next may come as a surprise to you. Even planning doesn't get anything accomplished (beyond the creation of a plan.) Nope. Not even planning. Only taking action.

Think about it. What was the last thing you absolutely had to accomplish? Did it get done? Ultimately, how did it happen? Someone took action.

If only taking action gets things done, is there any value to plans, goals, objectives, milestones, intentions, and all those other things we've been discussing? Yes.

The purpose of all those things is to help you figure out which actions to take, in what order, and when.

What about prayer, affirmations, or even wanting really badly? These things are certainly important to many people. You can probably point to instances where you "prayed for" or "affirmed" something and it happened.

This is outside the scope of this book, except to say that this type of self-communication can have a strong positive effect, add to your ability to motivate others, and intensify your own bias for action. In the end, however, it still boils down to taking action.

Leaders need to know this

In the final analysis, the job of a leader is to move people to action.
A leader may stir people up, get them wanting, or have them affirming.
A leader may have people praying or planning; setting goals, creating objec-
tives and declaring intentions. All important and all discussed at other
points in this book. Ultimately, a leader's job is to move people to take action.

Leaders tip:

If you absolutely, positively need to get something done—take action.

Yes—you should have clear commitments, objectives, goals, intentions and a plan. But to accomplish the result, you and your team need to be in action. Nothing else will do. And if you take action and the goal still isn't reached, take more action. And more, and more, and more.

Keep taking action until you've got it done.

Below is space to list 20 possible actions.

These actions will help you produce desired results and meet your objectives. Fill the page with all twenty. Throw away the worst 10 actions. Prioritize the rest. Start taking action.

_____   _____

_____   _____

_____   _____

_____   _____

_____   _____

_____   _____

_____   _____

_____   _____

_____   _____

_____   _____

Which important action can you take right now, this minute? Decide, and get moving.

67 ACCOUNTABILITY

You can count on me.
    Said by everyone who has ever accomplished anything worthwhile

Accountability is one of those words that cause a lot of confusion for people. It's really quite simple. Being accountable means you can be counted on to produce a specific outcome. You are the person people can depend on. You are the one they will turn to for success or failure.

You're the "Go-to guy."

That's what accountability means. No more, no less. When you are accountable, you are no longer a bystander or a spectator, but a full-fledged player.

Being accountable also means when your promises are not kept, you make new promises and suffer whatever the consequences are.

By accepting a position of leadership, you are saying "I am accountable for the team/group/company creating what it is says it will create." You are saying you will make sure the group honors its commitments and keeps its word.

In the end, accountability is about doing what you say you'll do.

DO SOMETHING. ANYTHING. 68

This chapter is a kind of intermezzo—a break in the action. This chapter is for those of you who still don't know what to do.

The answer? Do anything.

People get stuck trying to do things right. They want it to be perfect, and so do the task—whatever it is—over and over. They tweak it a little here, change something else there. Making it better and better, bit by bit, on and on.... Someday, they may decide it is finally ready for the grand debut.

Perfectionism is the death of many good opportunities. People fritter all of their lead time "getting it right" instead of bringing their venture out in the open and letting the market shape it.

The world already knows much more than you do about what will make your business great. People will be more than happy to tell you what's needed and wanted if you only expose yourself and your ideas to their opinions and thoughts.

The trick then, is to do something.

Just get into action.

You have a concept, an idea—do it now! Implement some version of your concept and get it out into the marketplace. Get feedback.

Perfect it in version two.

69 *FOLLOW THROUGH & FOLLOW UP*

It's true in golf, in baseball and in business; you have to follow through for truly great results.

Bad ideas don't lead to failure. Lack of follow-through leads to failure. Good ideas don't guarantee success. But good ideas plus great execution does.

Great execution is the key.

After all your values and vision and strategies and goals and game plans, what is left is taking action. And getting feedback and taking more action and getting feedback and taking even more action, and so on. That is called follow-through.

Create a project plan, with a time line and specific actions, the completion of which will likely implement your ideas. Do each of the actions—that is follow-through. If the plan goes astray, and it is clear it won't give you the results you seek, change the plan—and act on that one. That is follow-through. Keep going until you either succeed or deliberately abandon the project.

That is follow-through.

Typically your timing doesn't mesh perfectly with the people around you. An important customer isn't available when you call. You ask someone to do something—you have to check back with them, and take additional action. That is called follow-up.

Your venture's success may require hundreds, possibly thousands, of follow-up actions. Slipping up even a little bit will cause your business to suffer.

Have a tickler file for your follow-up actions. The form doesn't matter—write on a calendar or notebook, or use software. Develop the habit of putting all your follow-up items into a list and checking it regularly. Did you say you would get back to Kate on Wednesday?—then call her. Did you promise to send a case of your new fidgets to Jon by next week? Take care of it.

Better yet, send it early.

Timely and complete follow-up and follow-through is something people remember. They start to expect you to do the things you say you will, which raises the overall level of performance around your company. People will give you their best as a matter of course. That alone will cause your business to accelerate beyond your wildest expectations.

One more thing. If someone else makes a promise to you—and that promise is not fulfilled on time—make sure you follow up with them. Keep everyone on their toes. Expect top quality results. Expect people to keep their promises. This too will elevate the overall tone of your organization.

What three things should you follow through with or follow up on today?

1.

2.

3.

Okay... What are you waiting for?

70

What does it take to move mountains?
Faith, persistence, and the biggest shovel you can handle.

In <u>Think and Grow Rich</u>, Napoleon Hill says the surest way to grow rich is to have faith. But, he says, faith by itself will yield nothing. The secret is to have *"...faith backed by action. Action, action, action."*

This section is about massive action. Action, action, action. The surest way to get a lot done is to do a lot. Plan to do much more than you think is necessary for the accomplishment of your goals, then do it. Over plan everything. Over execute everything.

This approach guarantees your success.

If you think one hundred sales calls will get you there, make two hundred. Make a thousand. If you need three new ideas, don't stop until you have come up with ten. If you are writing five pages a day in your book, make it six, or seven. Make it ten. Twenty.

The least effort formula for success is: However much you are currently doing, do at least one more.

The payoff of massive action is easy to see in sports and the arts. The greatest basketball players spend the most time in practice. The greatest violinists play scales for hours on end. The greatest painters are often the most prolific.

This approach will give you tremendous results when you are launching a new venture. Massive action is an effective way to generate early momentum, and early momentum has a huge multiplier effect on your total results. Massive Action is also great when you are in a slump, when your results are down. Shift into high gear. Invoke the ten-to-one rule.

Commit yourself to massive action.

The most effort formula for success is: Put in at least 10 times the effort you think it should take.

You'll often hear that you should work smarter, not harder.

For truly outrageous results, why not do both?

Massive action = powerful results.

On the next page is a form you can use to invoke Massive Action. In what areas where you can use the most effort formula? Then note your typical run-rate, the average number of times you currently do these things. Now, come up with a new number—the massive action number. Commit to doing that number, whatever it is. Get in action.

| Area for Massive Action | Current Run Rate

How many of these things do you do each day, week or month? | Massive Action Rate

How many you will do in the next day, week or month? | What results will this produce? | When will you get started? |
|---|---|---|---|---|
| | | | | |
| | | | | |
| | | | | |
| | | | | |
| | | | | |
| | | | | |
| | | | | |

Whatever your plan calls for, do more.

Whenever your plan calls for something, do it sooner.

One sure way to create breakthroughs is to pour it on. Think of pouring it on in terms of action and reaction. Pouring it on means not only taking more actions of a single kind, but taking far more action than you've ever taken. It means taking those actions faster and faster.

It also means decreasing your reaction time. Shortening the gaps between when something needs to happen and when it happens.

If you speed up each action, and you do more of it, and you shorten your reaction time—the effect will not be merely additive or even multiplicative; it will exponentially increases the velocity of your results. If you double the output of process A, and then you double process B which works on process A...

You get the idea.

You can't keep this up indefinitely, of course. If need quick results though—perhaps for morale, perhaps for investors—pour it on. Demonstrate dramatic performance.

Pick your spot. Select an area in the venture, and pour it on. Double your targets, move up your milestone.

Clear your decks and get busy.

72 *BIG DIFFERENCES*

Focus on the key points.

Train yourself to identify what is important. Think in terms of high impact, and set your sights on areas where the biggest differences will be made. Skip the trivia.

Whenever you must make a decision about resources, or select among possible actions—ask which will make the biggest difference. Not what will be easier, or more fun, or take less time. The things which are easier, or more fun or take less time may make the biggest difference because of those same characteristics, just don't make your selection that way. Think of the greatest influence on your venture. Where is the maximum payback? The biggest contribution?

Ask which actions are worth the effort you'll expend on them.

What resource allocations will put you closest to your goal? Those are the right choices to make. If the likely result is marginal, find something else to do with your time. Go for the big differences.

If you sweat the small stuff, you'll spend all your time sweating.

Do this:

Make a list of five things you are currently working on which are not likely to pay big dividends.

_____

_____

_____

_____

_____

One by one, examine why you are doing these things. If it is not because of the direct effect it has on your top-most priorities, is there some other reason? Is there some hidden future benefit that is motivating you, that when considered makes this thing important?
If not...

STOP DOING THESE THINGS, RIGHT NOW.

Make another list of five things you aren't working on, each of which would make a difference if you were.

_____

_____

_____

_____

_____

Take action on at least two of these things immediately.

73   *A GAME WORTH PLAYING*

You play, you get paid.

In his book, <u>The Game of Work</u>, Charles Coonradt said that if people think something is a game, not only will they pay for the privilege of working harder, they will work much harder than when they are themselves getting paid.

Don't think that's so? Take golf. Or a bit of one-on-one basketball. Both of these sports require more physical effort and skill than most of our 9-5 pursuits. Then there's chess, which consumes more calories of concentrated brainpower than most people's jobs.

What makes something a game?

All games have several things in common. As you go through this list, think of games you have played, *(at least those you can identify as such)*, and compare each of these characteristics to your business.

◙   Games have pre-defined objective outcomes—goals.
Golf has eighteen holes and strokes under or over par. Basketball has baskets at two or three points each. Chess has checkmate. Tag has, well, tag. Plus, each of these objectives— well arguably not tag, but then you are most likely older than ten—are challenging.

It isn't much of a game when it's easy to reach the goals.

◙   Games have a fixed time frame, and all the players know what that frame is. Even golf—the game will be called on account of darkness.

- Games have boundaries which delineate the field of play. The players need to know what's fair and what's foul.

- Games have rules which prescribe what are acceptable and unacceptable actions. The field of play, and what the goal is. All the players know what they are.

- Games have players and teams, all of whom are volunteers. And—this is very important—everyone knows who is on their team and who is on the other team.

- Games have rewards for winning. Ever play a game with some one who says they don't care whether they win or not? It's kind of annoying, isn't it? Of course your team wants to win.

- All the defining elements of games—goals, duration, what's fair and what's foul, the rules, who's on what team, what the rewards are—are public information. All the players are supposed to have a shared understanding of these things.

- Games are fun. If it's not fun, it's not a game.

People like to play games.

We've been doing it since childhood, and we're happy to do it now. How many times have you heard people who love their work say, "It's like a game to me." And people definitely work harder at games. Think about the effort people put into skiing, or playing football, or bridge.

If it isn't a game already, turn your business into one. What do you need to add to make your business a game? Let's go through the list.

FASTER THAN THE SPEED OF CHANGE

Have a set of well-defined objectives—make sure they are clear to all the players—and make sure those objectives are challenging. *(If they weren't, you'd probably try to find another game to play.)*

Align your players into teams. Set time frames. Define the rules of engagement. Establish the rewards for winning.

Make it a game worth playing.

Above all, make it fun.

How do you know if you're winning?

What is the first thing you look at on a map? If you are like me, you locate where you currently are, and then you locate the place you are going—or vice versa. You have to do these things—after all, how can you chart a course to somewhere else, when you don't know where you are?

The same thing is true for all runaway ventures. You must know where you stand now and you must know where you are headed. Plus you need a way to mark your progress and your performance.

The metrics in a system tell you lots of important things. Well defined metrics tell you where you are at any time, in any terms you define. Where you are in profits, sales, production, new hires, geographic expansion, education, skill level, even the number of cookies baked—you name it. Those same metrics let you establish goals, and put timeframes on them. How many will you accomplish, by when?

A measurement system is how you keep score.

It's a way to tell whether you should go faster or slower; whether you should increase production or back off.

It's been said that the fastest way to affect any aspect of any venture is to measure it. Just by setting up a tracking system you will improve your effectiveness in a given area. Try it.

Also, if you ask someone to be accountable for producing a specific result, you need a way to measure whether that result is being produced. If the result is going to occur over a long enough period of time, you need interim results to see if they are on track or require corrective action.

Without measurements, you'll never know if you're winning. Without that, what's the point of the game?

Anything can be measured

There are six keys to setting up an effective measurement system.

▣ The measures must be easy to understand and interpret. Let people know how your measures are constructed.

▣ The measures must be tested before you roll them out. Do they actually measure what you want them to? Are your measures sensitive to tweaking the process? Do they respond to changes you make?

▣ Measures should be cost effective and low impact. You don't want to create lots of additional work to get your measurements.

▣ Only measure things which provide high leverage.

▣ The results must be available quickly, ideally in real time. A long enough time lag between actions and results will kill any measurement program.

▣ If you are asking people to measure themselves, provide feed back from the measurements even more quickly.

HOW TO IMPROVE ANYTHING 75

Creating breakthrough improvements is easier than you think.

To do this, simply define your goals, establish measurements of their success, and take action to make those goals reality.

Here's the 6 step process to make this happen:

1. Decide what factors are critical to the success of your venture.

2. Establish a set of measurements for each factor, with a target value for each metric.

3. Set a timeframe for that target value to be reached.

4. Develop a procedure for gathering the data.

5. Now, invent high-leverage initiatives to impact that critical success factor, and upgrade the metric values. Put the whole thing into action and keep score.

6. Examine your results often, and make as many changes as necessary to keep the whole process functioning well and on track.

Looked at as a whole, even this might seem intimidating. To see how easy it really is, pick one area you'd like to improve. Start with something small. Then work through the steps, in order.

You're in for a pleasant surprise.

76   *BEING UNSTOPPABLE*

What would it be like to be unstoppable?

Do you know anyone you would call unstoppable? Someone who never stopped at anything. Never got stuck. Someone who was always moving forward towards their heart's desires, no matter what?

Can you see yourself that way?

What if, no matter what happened, no matter what got in your way, you simply could not be stopped. That you would move Heaven and Earth to accomplish the object of your commitment. If you were that kind of person, would that get you to where you wanted to go a whole lot faster than the ordinary you?

Of course it would. But how do you get that way?

Go back to that person you know. What makes them unstoppable? What are they like? Does everything just go their way? Of course not! Do they really never get stuck? Of course they do! What makes them unstoppable is one very simple thing.

They don't stay stuck for very long.

You and I—it could take us a long time to realize we are stuck. Then it takes more time to figure out what to do about it. Sometimes we wallow around wondering why things aren't going as planned. How did things ever get this way, anyway? Unstoppable people don't stay stuck; they train themselves to figure things out quickly. When they get stuck they notice right away. That's the whole secret to being unstoppable.

Here's the magic formula for becoming unstoppable

◉ Stop.

◉ Notice that you are stopped.

◉ Acknowledge that you are stopped.

◉ Get support from a committed listener.
  (This step is optional but it really helps.)

◉ Invent a whole raft of possible actions to take right now, to get things moving again.

◉ Take those actions.

Now you're unstopped.

People who are committed to being unstoppable simply get themselves back in action as soon as they realize they aren't.

Make your reaction time shorter. Learn to make adjustments quickly. Become aware. Become adaptable.

Become unstoppable.

77   *BEING UNSTOPPABLE—PART 2: MOVING THROUGH IT*

Where you are stuck?

What you can do about it?

On the left side below, list 2 specific areas where you are stopped. (Stuck, stopped, mired, not moving forward, quit...). Then, on the right side, list 5 actions which would move that area forward towards the results you are committed to.

1. _____

     a. _____
     b. _____
     c. _____
     d. _____
     e. _____

2. _____

     a. _____
     b. _____
     c. _____
     d. _____
     e. _____

Move on one or more of these actions right now.
Get un-stopped.

BREAKDOWNS 78

Breakdown: an interruption in what you had planned.

When your car gets a flat tire on your way to Grandma's, you call it a breakdown. (Note that if your car gets a flat in the garage, you do not call it a breakdown.) What's special about this kind of breakdown is that you call attention to it. You make a formal statement noting your breakdown. You say—I'm having a breakdown with such-and-such.

Perhaps you aren't making sufficient progress in an area—you aren't moving fast enough. Maybe your results are just different from what you expected, or things are plain off track.

Since this might seem like familiar territory for you, let's add a little twist. This kind of breakdown is not really a bad thing. An acquaintance of mine had the saying, "Breakdowns lead to break-throughs," and you can expect to have them from time to time. In fact, if you are not experiencing breakdowns on a regular basis, what you are doing isn't much of a stretch.

Notice I didn't say a breakdown is when things go wrong.

Breakdowns are not problems—they are just you not getting the results you planned, when you planned for them.

Train yourself to make formal declarations of breakdowns: *"There is a breakdown in such-and-such."* This gives you a chance to stop the action, take a breath, see what's up, and invent what to do next. That's different from—*"Uh-oh, somebody must have screwed up...."* Or, *"Things are all messed up. I hope no one finds out"*, and *"How can we get out of this?"*

People normally keep it to themselves when they notice things aren't going the way they think they should be going. This only makes matters worse. If things are off track and nothing gets done about it for a while, does that usually make matters better or worse? Wouldn't you rather "come clean" immediately and figure out what to do about it? In the breakdown process no one is blamed or found lacking.

Being off course isn't personal, it's just off course.

Declaring a breakdown is also a chance to reexamine how you are doing things, and tweak the process from time to time.

Train the people you work with to use breakdowns. Let them know breakdowns are OK—that you won't hit them over the head or shame them in public. Declare breakdowns quickly so you have a way to get back on course quickly. This is one of the secrets to getting where you want to go quickly.

This is a key to becoming unstoppable.

The breakdown process

Here's a simple process to follow when you notice you aren't making progress in an area, or are otherwise off course.

1. Use the following or similar words: "There is a breakdown in such and such."

2. Describe the facts of the situation. What happened, exactly. Leave out what you think was good and what was bad, and all your justifications about why you let things get that way. Stick to the facts.

3. What were you trying to accomplish that got interrupted? What precisely is off track? Are you still committed to that?

4. What are the objectives and measures for realizing that commitment? (These can be the same as before or all new ones.)

5. Design actions that will have you meet those objectives.

6. Get back in action.

Simple as changing a flat. And just as effective in getting you moving again.

79   *THE LIST OF ONE HUNDRED*

Take out several sheets of paper and make a list of 100 ways to get to your next milestone.

How many did you really write? Did you list 100 ways? What about 10 ways? The average person writes six ways. I challenge you to go the distance and write all 100. Some of the ways will be silly, some of them might be ridiculous.

Some of them could forever alter the course of your life.

Could you make a list of 100 ways to promote your venture in the community? Or a list of 100 ways to deliver outstanding service to your customers? Or 100 ways to cut your expenses or increase profits? Or a hundred ways to get key appointments? What if you made a list of 100 new product ideas, or a little easier, 100 ways to enhance your existing product?

How about a list of 100 factors which could impact your success in any way at all?

Or a list of 100 "dream clients?" Couple that list with a list of 100 ways to get those clients and you've got a breakthrough for sure.

Write your list of 100.

When you are done writing all 100, take the 20 best ideas. Set to work one at a time.

That should keep you busy.

Never give up. Never, never, never give up.

Winston Churchill

Here's a success tip if there ever was one:

Don't Quit.

This elegant tip has such potency, it could single-handedly change your entire world. I could stop here and make this the shortest chapter in the book.

But couple "Don't Quit," and "Just Do It," and you got the complete success formula in five economical words.

It has been said that the only real failure comes from quitting before the job is done. If that is true, you can guarantee a successful outcome by vowing never to quit. It is totally in your control. Never to stop doing until your aims are realized.

Legend says that Thomas Edison tried 10,000 separate filaments for the incandescent light bulb before finding one that did the job. Do you have that kind of stamina? Are you willing to go the distance?

Do you care that much?

Think of the power not quitting would bring to you. Imagine that you knew, no matter what, you would keep going until you got wherever it was you set out for. What kind of confidence would that lend to your efforts? Would that change the way you related to people? Would it alter the way you asked people for things?

What if things took at turn for the worse? Would you be crushed, or would you simply take things in stride and keep going?

Think this over first, because you don't want to make a declaration of so much power and then renege on it. See if you are willing to make this kind of commitment, and if so, declare that

"For me, with respect to _____ *(fill in the blank)*, quitting is not an option."

DO THE RIGHT THING **81**

You make decisions. You make choices. You take action.

Sometimes you will be right and sometimes you will be wrong. Sometimes other people will be right. Can you live with that?

Can you handle being wrong?

To make your business soar past the competition, you must master right action. That is, you must develop a constant concern with making the right choices—whatever that may mean to you—especially after you've just made the wrong ones. Give up insisting on being right.

The problem with "being right" is that if you are, in fact, wrong, wanting to be right will keep you from doing the right thing.

Wanting to look as if you were right all along will cause you to justify your actions, defend your position, and challenge the correctness of other people's points of view. You won't be able to accept that you have made a mistake, so you won't be able to take corrective action. You will get caught up in all sorts of arguments, finger pointing, and head games to make the people around you seem wrong instead.

If you develop a concern with doing the right thing it will be easy for you simply admit you are wrong.

Then take steps to fix it.

82

REQUISITE VARIETY

Variety is the spice of life.

The principle of requisite variety says that a species survives to the exact degree that it is able to adopt new behaviors.

Most of us have a set of standard responses to situations that arise. When one of our buttons gets pressed we typically have the button A response ready. Or the button B response. This makes it easy for us to "handle" things.

Remember that famous definition of insanity—doing the same things over and expecting a different response.

Our standard responses keep us from creating breakthroughs. If we always do the same thing, we are likely to stay in the same loops. Breakthroughs require that we invoke the law of requisite variety and get flexible.

Purposely seek to generate new behaviors. Deliberately look for different ways to do things, especially when it becomes clear that our old ways aren't working as well as they used to.

Can you identify habitual responses you have? For instance, when you miss a sales goal, do you automatically decide to do start a new business campaign? If quarterly revenues are off, do you reflexively seek to cut expenses?

The ropes that tie us down are often woven of slender threads of habit.

Be aware of these habits.

Do this:

Take a sheet of paper and draw columns as below.

Identify four situations where you typically react with a set response. Then identify two new possible approaches to use the next time one of those situations occurs.

Situation   Habitual response   New approach

83

The harder you hold on to things, the faster they can get away from you.

If you want to extend your reach beyond your ability to do everything at once, you must delegate some things to other people.

Delegation is frightening for many people. First of all, you might enjoy doing the thing you have to delegate. You may think you do it better than anyone else. You imagine it won't get done properly. And you know it won't get done your way. You might even believe if you don't do that thing, you won't have enough to do.

Know this: whatever you keep to yourself instead of delegating will get shorter shrift than it deserves. Usually that thing becomes a bottleneck in the continued success of your venture.

There are four keys to effective delegating.

1. Give the job to someone who can get it done—someone who either has, or has access to, the skills, knowledge and resources needed. Also, give the job to someone who has time for it. Don't dump your projects onto someone who has neither the where-withal nor the availability.

If you do that you are simply setting them up to fail and setting yourself up for disappointment. Don't just hand your task to the next warm body. Get buy-in from the delegate. Are they okay with this thing? Are they enrolled, or is this just more work for someone who is already overburdened?

2. Communicate your conditions of satisfaction. Have you ever asked someone to do something, and when they came back you said, "Oh. That's not what I wanted at all"? Be sure you have mutual agreement on the critical requirements that define how this job must be handled, and what the outcome will look like.

Use SMART goals to clarify the desired outcome along with a timeline for its realization. Also, if necessary, set up a measurement system that will help you and your delegate know whether things are on or off track.

3. Work out a plan. Depending on the complexity of the delegated task, you may ask that the first step be a plan for how to get the rest done. In other cases, the request may be simple and a plan not necessary. But think this through.

If you are uncertain as to how something needs to get done, but want to make sure it will occur according to some guidelines—get a plan.

4. Finally, you need a communications protocol—how are you going to get updates and give feedback or advice? When are you going to speak or meet? How frequently? Will they send you an email, or a formal progress report? Create some pre-defined mechanism to keep you informed, and to give them an opportunity to seek guidance if appropriate.

There is a big difference between delegating and abdicating. When you abdicate you are saying—I'm neither responsible nor accountable for the results. When you delegate, you are still accountable. You are asking your delegate to do the work, and therefore be accountable to you.

"Never tell people how to do things. Tell them what to do and they will surprise you with their ingenuity."

General George S. Patton

84 *TRACKING SYSTEMS*

If you can't track it, don't do it.

Every high-performance venture needs a tracking system. A tracking system lets everyone know how well they are doing relative to their commitments. It is a guide to whether additional or extraordinary actions need to be taken.

Without an objective tracking system it is hard for people to be clear about their results.

Establish intentions for your project, determine suitable measurements to quantify and qualify those intentions, and set performance goals for those measures. For example, your intention is to increase market penetration. The measure is your venture's sales divided by total sales in your market. The baseline is your current market share of 10%, and you have targeted 25% by the end of the year.

That's objective, measurable, and thus—achievable.

Have someone be accountable for your project's performance measured against each intention. Establish a timely tracking system for each measure, which easily gathers the necessary data. Develop periodic interim performance goals, and a reporting structure to let everyone involved know how they are doing.

Your performance tracking systems can be kept with pen and paper, or they can be automated on your computer system. However you implement them, keep it simple and don't let the overhead of your tracking system become a burden of any kind.

On the next page is a very simple system I used to keep track of my output while writing this book. It was kept on a computer spreadsheet, but could just as easily been pencil on graph paper.

Whenever I was "below the line" I had catching up to do.

Example Tracking Graph

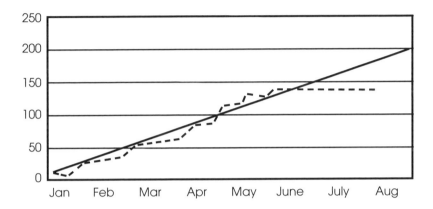

Start with 0 in the lower left corner, write units of measurement along the left axis, and dates of measurement along the bottom. Draw a straight reference line from 0 to your goal, and plot your performance against that goal. Of course the reference line need not be straight; set it up in whatever way reflects the time-relationship of your goals.

Determine to stay above the line.

It's an amazingly simple way to keep focused.

EPILOGUE

In these pages I have written much about building a higher performance venture, creating breakthroughs, inventing the future and moving faster than the speed of change.

The most important thing you can do now—right at this moment—is get moving. Reading this book and simply setting it down, even if you say to yourself "Wow! That sounds like it will work!" will, unfortunately, accomplish nothing.

Pick a problem and apply the ideas that you think fit that problem best.

Or pick a chapter at random and put it to work.

You needn't start big (although that would be my personal preference)—start small if you like. Choose an idea and use it in your next management meeting. Or take a concept and apply it to that thorny sales problem you have. Perhaps some of your employees can be supercharged by a particular chapter. Start anywhere, start doing anything, but start.

If you want a breakthrough, you must first decide to create it.

If you want to shape the future, you must see its possibility in your mind's eye.

If you want to move faster than change, you must be fluid, flexible, willing to change your "mind" on a moments notice and committed to staying in action.

Then you have to get busy and make it happen. I hope I've given you some tools with which to do that . They have worked for many of my clients, I believe they will work for you.

My email address is paul@lemberg.com. My office phone is (760)741-1747.

I'd be thrilled to hear about the future you create for yourself and your company.

Well? What are you doing just sitting there?

Get moving... Faster than the speed of change!

Paul Lemberg

ABOUT THE AUTHOR

Paul Lemberg is an executive coach, futurist, strategist and speaker. He has consulted with executives from companies such as Goldman Sachs, Lexis/Nexis, American Skandia, OpenText, Mass Mutual, SAIC, JP Morgan, and Solomon Software. He is the founder of Lemberg & Company, a coaching, technology forecasting, and breakthrough strategy firm, serving high tech, finance, biotech and other fast-track businesses. As a speaker and coach, Paul has worked with thousands of executives and entrepreneurs to have more profitable, productive and satisfying businesses: to be more effective executives, leaders, managers, strategists and entrepreneurs. Prior to starting Lemberg & Company, Paul co-founded, and later sold, two international banking software companies, a multimedia production company, and a sales training company. Later, as a market researcher and product strategist, Paul worked with major technology companies including Texas Instruments, Compaq, EDS, Anderson Consulting, IBM, KPMG, MCI and Bell Atlantic.

Paul's executive letter, "Extraordinary Results," is read by over twenty thousand people in over forty countries. He is a popular speaker at conferences in the U.S. and Canada, focusing on topics relating to executive coaching and leadership, the future of technology and how technology affects your business and industry future.

Paul has a bicameral education: he studied fine arts as an undergrad and international finance and marketing as a graduate student. In 1975, he helped found an art gallery in Buffalo, N.Y., and worked on pioneering computer-generated video and music. Since then, he has been a software designer, market researcher and technology forecaster, international marketing and sales director, corporate strategist, technology guru and chief executive. He serves on the Board of the San Diego High-Tech Marketing Association and is a founding member of the International Consortia of Business Coaches.